THE FIRST SEVEN DAYS
A Philosophical Commentary
on the Creation of Genesis

SOUTH FLORIDA STUDIES IN THE HISTORY OF JUDAISM

Edited by
Jacob Neusner
William Scott Green, James Strange
Darrell J. Fasching, Sara Mandell

Number 61
The First Seven Days
A Philosophical Commentary
on the Creation of Genesis

by
Norbert M. Samuelson

THE FIRST SEVEN DAYS

A Philosophical Commentary
on the Creation of Genesis

by
Norbert M. Samuelson

Scholars Press
Atlanta, Georgia

THE FIRST SEVEN DAYS
A Philosophical Commentary on the Creation of Genesis

©1992
University of South Florida

Publication of this book was made possible by a grant from the Tisch Family Foundation, New York City. The University of South Florida acknowledges with thanks this important support for its scholarly projects.

Library of Congress Cataloging in Publication Data

Samuelson, Norbert Max, 1936-
　　The first seven days : a philosophical commentary on the creation of Genesis / by Norbert M. Samuelson.
　　p. cm. — (South Florida studies in the history of Judaism ; 61)
　　Includes bibliographical references and index.
　　ISBN 1-55540-768-4 (alk. paper)
　　1. Creation—Biblical teaching. 2. Bible. O.T. Genesis I, 1-II, 3—Criticism, interpretation, etc. I. Title. II. Series.
BS651.S3165 1992
222'.1106—dc20　　　　　　　　　　　　　　　92-32166
　　　　　　　　　　　　　　　　　　　　　　　CIP

Printed in the United States of America
on acid-free paper

To

Annie

My OR CHADASH

Table of Contents

Preface 1

Part I: The Physics of Creation

Day 0 (Gen 1:1-2) 7
Day 1 (Gen 1:3-5) 25
Day 2 (Gen 1:6-8) 41
Day 3 (Gen 1:9-13) 53

Part II: The Politics of Creation

Day 4 (Gen 1:14-19) 75
Day 5 (Gen 1:20-23) 91
Day 6 (Gen 1:24-31) 109
Day 7 (Gen 2:1-3) 139

Conclusion 149
Appendix: An Outline of Gen 1:1-2:3 155
Bibliography 165
Indices 179
    Greek & Latin Terms 179
    Hebrew Terms 179
    Names & Books 180
    Biblical Names & Books 181
    Subjects 181

PREFACE

This book is an in-depth, logical analysis of the concept of creation contained in the original Hebrew text of the first thirty-four verses of the Book of Genesis. As such, the methodology employed is somewhat original. Hence, a few words of explanation are in order.

This book is a study of the Hebrew Scriptures that differs from, but is influenced by, the critical source/historical and literary approaches in the contemporary academic study of the Bible, the theological orientation in close textual readings in medieval Jewish philosophical commentaries, and the contemporary methods of conceptual text analysis in both Anglo-American and in continental philosophy. In agreement with the medieval commentators, this study assumes that the biblical text contains philosophy, i.e., it makes claims about many (if not all) of the classical subjects of philosophical speculation. (Notably in terms of Genesis 1, the areas of philosophy include physics and political science.) Furthermore, those judgments are in some sense authoritative for all committed Jews and Christians in determining what it is they believe as Jews and Christians. However, unlike them, no attempt is made here to read Scripture apologetically. While there is no way to avoid the influence of one's religious and cultural traditions in reading the familiar words of Scripture, every attempt is made to minimize that background. (In my case, the tradition is rabbinic, and my personal commitment is to liberal Judaism.) In other words, the text is allowed to speak for itself to as great an extent as is possible. The intended result is a determination of the literal meaning of the text, whether or not that meaning conforms to any past interpretations or shared dogmas in any biblically-based religious community, as well as whether or not that meaning agrees with any preconceived notions of what the text should say. In this sense the "spirit" of interpretation in this book is that of contemporary continental philosophy. As in phenomenology, setting aside prejudices (both scholarly and religious) is imperative. And, as in both deconstruction and postmodernism, analysis consists largely in breaking down the meaning of phrases into their words, which in turn are broken down into their etymological bases. However, the method of analysis employed here has more in common with the philosophic tradition of linguistic analysis than it does with any form of continental philosophy in its emphasis on both conceptual precision and its reliance on common sense.

Finally, in agreement with contemporary academic historical studies of the Bible, the text is read as if it were a human document, written and edited in a particular place at a particular time. As such, it can in principle make claims that are either incoherent or false. However, unlike the standard work of biblical historians, no attempt is made the sort out different stratums of the text into documents produced at different times in different places. (In my opinion, the attempt by modern source critical biblical historians to differentiate historical layers of the text based on apparent conceptual contradictions is only a modern variation on the appeals of medieval biblical commentators to multiple metaphorical levels in interpretation to reconcile what they believed to be incoherent.) Rather, in keeping with the way modern literary critics read the text, the focus on an author — i.e., the one or ones through whom the text is speaking — is more on an editor of the hypothesized different pieces than it is on the writers of the pieces themselves. To use an analogy, the text of Genesis is read here as the work of the editors rather than as the work of the authors edited, in the way that a motion picture can be discussed as the work of its director or producers rather than the author of the novel upon which the screen play was based, the writers of the screen play, the cameramen, the film editors, et. al. Specifically in terms of the first chapter of Genesis, the "author" is assumed to be the Judean priests who resided in Babylonia during the first exile, rather than the authors of E, J, or any other possible historical sources that contemporary biblical scholars claim as the original authors. In this respect, the methodology employed in this book is neutral as to authorship. In other words, the method of analysis is intended to unpack what the text itself says, independent of what was the historical intention of the author, be that author God (as most Jewish traditionalists and Christian fundamentalists would maintain) or editors of the entire Bible in the second Jewish state during its Hellenistic period, or the Jewish priests who produced the Pentateuch during the first Babylonian exile. In other words, the goal is to deduce a "best reading" of the text. Now, if a best reading is found and God is the author, then it would follow that the determined meaning is what God intended. However, if the author(s) are human, this need not be the case. In other words, given human authorship, a best reading certainly would have something in common with the intended meaning. However, a best reading can contain elements of which the author was in fact unaware but should have been aware.

The employment of the methodology of this book results in a number of significant conclusions. The first has to do with the legitimate range of possible interpretations. The text is relatively ambiguous. Of course, that it is imprecise is to be expected. Rather, the surprise is that the account of creation is not *absolutely* equivocal, i.e., there are significant limits on what may or may not count as a valid interpretation of the meaning of creation in Genesis. Among the kind of views that legitimately fall within the range of possible interpretations are general cosmologies based on contemporary astrophysics. The same cannot be said for most so-called literal interpretations of the Bible by many American, Protestant, so-called fundamentalists, whose reading of Scripture depends on a Christian tradition of translating the text into European languages. This translation tradition has produced a number of readings that lie beyond the scope of possible interpretations of the original intent of the Hebrew text, e.g., that creation is a temporal event that occurs over the course of the first seven days of our present material universe. In general, the disparate readings are the ones most in conflict with modern scientific theory. In other words, a careful reading of the Hebrew text of Genesis would suggest that what most contemporary scientists say about the origin of the universe is closer to what the Hebrew Bible actually says than what many Christian biblical literalists call the Bible's doctrine of creation.

The second has to do with the kind of philosophical claims that are implicit in the Hebrew Bible's narration of the origin of the universe. What emerges from a logical analysis of the biblical text is an ontology that shares a number of features with Plato's *Timaeus* . Some of these similarities have a long history in Western European philosophy, e.g., the use of mathematical models to order the seemingly unintelligible, unending flux of concrete existence. At the same time, there are other philosophical similarities between these two works — often expounded in the philosophical traditions of Asia and the Mediterranean — that stand in marked contrast to the dominant Western philosophic tradition of ontology, e.g., the primacy of substances over relations (i.e., actors over actions), positivism over negativism (i.e., what is something over what is nothing), and what occupies space over the space itself.

Finally, I understand this biblical commentary to be a study *in* religious philosophy rather than a study *about* the philosophy of religion. I do not plan to debate methodology in this work. However, many readers will recognize that the approach used here presupposes particular, somewhat subtle, stands on many issues about how to do religious philosophy. For example, these readers will have trouble fitting me into either the British tradition of logical analysis or the continental tradition of hermeneutics, although they should recognize the influence of both on this work. Similarly, readers who identify with contemporary efforts to draw a sharp separation between theology and religious philosophy will recognize that I am not among them.

To summarize, the body of this book is a simple reading in detail — word by word, and sentence by sentence — of the standard masoretic Hebrew edition of Genesis 1:1 through 2:3. The text is treated as a single entity. The form of analysis is philosophical rather than literary or historical. Furthermore, the concern in reading the text is its meaning on its own. No use is made of other manuscripts from the ancient Near East to interpret it, and no attempt is made to reconcile any apparent contradictions by an appeal to different sources of the biblical text itself. In other words, the intent we are trying to discover is that of the editors and not of any individuals who may have written material that the editors incorporated into their final version of the text. There are some allusions to comparable cosmologies and cosmogonies in other parts of the standard masoretic edition of the Hebrew Scriptures, on the assumption that both texts have the same editors. However, since the first thirty-four verses are treated as a distinct work, such allusions play a minor role in reading the primary text.

The conclusion is a description of a concept of the origin and general nature of the universe that forms a critical part of the theology by which biblical Judaism, i.e., the (pre-rabbinic) Judaism of the editors of the Hebrew Scriptures, interpreted its universe. If the analysis presented in this book is correct, then subsequent theologies in Hellenistic Judaism (including that of the earliest rabbis) should be understood as a response to and/or reaction against this theology. The final chapter attempts to move beyond description to critical judgment about what is true about the conception of the origin and nature of the universe in the Hebrew Scriptures. This final enterprise presupposes that creation is a religious doctrine to which truth judgments are appropriate, and that making such judgments involves a serious confrontation between the past (as reflected in traditional religious texts) and the present (as reflected in the best academic research related to the subject in question).

DAY 0

This study is a philosophical analysis of the account of creation in the first thirty four verses of the Book of Genesis. By "analysis" I mean what others might call a "close reading," i.e., a detailed — word by word, phrase by phrase, line by line — examination of the language of the text. By "philosophical" I mean two things. First, the primary interest in the text is its conceptual content, not its literary form or its historical significance. This is not to say that these other perspectives will be entirely ignored. On the contrary, they will play a significant role in determining, as precisely as the words themselves allow, what the content is. Second, the text will be interpreted, at least at this initial stage of analysis, primarily in terms of its internal logic, i.e., its formal coherence and consistency, independent of its relation to other bodies of literature. In other words, a veil of ignorance (to borrow a phrase from John Rawls[1]) will be imposed on the reading. So that the words may speak for themselves, as free as possible from imposed presuppositions from associations with other works, no attempt will be made here to see (or even think of) this text in relationship to parallel creation stories within the Hebrew Scriptures themselves[2] or to the wide variety of

---

[1] John Rawls. *A Theory of Justice*. Cambridge (MA), Harvard University Press, 1971.

[2] There are multiple references to creation in the Hebrew Scriptures. The more extensive accounts can be found in Gen 1:1-2:3, Ex 40:12-25, Ps 74:12-17, Ps 104:1-35, Job 26:7-14, and Job 38:4-39:30. The so-called "second creation story," Gen 2:4-3:24, has nothing to do with "creation" in the sense in which we are using the word. Rather, it deals with the beginning of human life after the physical creation has taken place. In fact the only part of the second account that directly relates to the first is Gen 2:7, with reference to Gen 1:26-27, on the creation of the human being ("HA-ADAM").

Genesis 1:1

בראשית ברא אלהים את השמים ואת הארץ:
Be-RESHIT BARA ELOHIM ET HA-SHAMAYIM Ve-ET HA-ARETZ
To begin with, God gods the sky and the (planet) earth.

"Be" is a preposition, and, like most prepositions, it can be translated as many other prepositions in any other language, depending on what it means in context. Hence, "Be" can mean "at," "in," "by," "from," "with," etc., depending on its function in connection with RESHIT and the rest of the sentence.

"RESHIT" almost always[3] is the construct form of "RISHON" or "RISHONAH." In the English language, no grammatical distinction is made between the construct and absolute forms of a noun, i.e., between the way a word is uttered when it stands by itself (the absolute state) and the way it is uttered when it stands in relationship to another word as something possessed. For example, the word "house" has the same form in the sentence "The house is large," where the term "house" is absolute, as it does in the sentence, "The house of John is large," where the term is in a construct state. In contrast, the term for a house has a different form in the Hebrew equivalents of these two sentences. The first sentence would be "HA-BAYIT HU GADOL." Syntactically, the sentence says, "The-house it large." "The" is the Hebrew consonant "H" added to the noun for house in its absolute form("BAYIT"). The verb "to be" has no expression in the present tense within the declarative

---

[3] The two exceptions in the Pentateuch are Lev 2:12 and Dt 33:21, where the term means " a first (fruit)" in the absolute state. However, in both of these cases it is possible to read the text as saying "a first of (fruit)" where the absolute term (fruit) that the construct term (first) modifies is assumed contextually without being explicitly stipulated. Parallel ambiguity is involved in the other cases in the Hebrew Scriptures where the term "RESHIT" appears grammatically in an absolute state, viz., Neh 12:44, Ps 105:36 (where "RESHIT" explicitly is a synonymn for first-produce ["BeKHOR"]), and Isa 46:10 (the first of [time]).

sentence. Instead, a personal pronoun (viz., "HU") is inserted to express the relation declared between the predicate expression ("GADOL") and the subject expression ("HA-BAYIT"). The second sentence would be "BET YONATAN HU GADOL." "BET" is the word for house in its construct state. In this sentence it means "the house of ...," but it could also mean "a house of ..." The suffix letter, H, that makes its noun definite, drops out in the case of a noun in its construct form. Hence, you can only tell if the reference is definite (viz., "the") or indefinite (viz., "a" or "an") by context. Therefore, "RESHIT" means, "a or the RISHONAH of ..."

Most Hebrew terms have a three consonant root, and the fact that different words share the same root often indicates that they share some meaning. The terms "RISHON" and "RISHONAH" share with the term "ROSH" the root letters resh (ר), aleph (א), and shin (ש). The shared meaning is, being first in some respect. When the frame of reference is a person's body, "ROSH" usually means "head," i.e., what is first with respect to spatial position, viz., at the top. However, as the English expression, "at the top" need not always have a spatial reference, so the term "ROSH" need not always have a spatial reference. For example, "at the top of the class" or "at the head of the class" can mean first with respect to quality or first with respect to achievement, and have nothing to do with any kind of spatial reference. As with "ROSH," so with "RISHON" and "RISHONAH." All three words, depending on their context, refer to something that is first in some respect, but the relevant respect is determined solely by the rest of the linguistic context. If the reference framework is one of value, then these terms express what is best. If the framework is one of quantity, then they express what is biggest. If the framework is a linear ordering, then they express an origin, i.e., an initial item. Hence, "the first of time" would be either the first time (with respect to linear ordering) or the chief time, where "the chief" could mean "most of the" (with respect to quantity) or "the most important" (with respect to quality). However, the framework need not be time at all.

Interpretation would be much easier if the first term of the text were "BA-RISHONAH" rather than "Be-RESHIT." Within the context of Genesis 1:1 it would say, "at first." Of course, the phrase's meaning still would be ambiguous. "At first" also need not be a temporal reference. Its sense could just as well be logical. Similarly, "at first" need not have any reference at all; it may only function contextually, like "once upon a time," to say that this is the beginning of the story. However, at least it would make some kind of sense within the sentence. For "Be-RESHIT" to have any clear meaning it would have to be followed by a noun in the absolute state. Alas, it is not. The next term is a verb. As such it would seem either that some word is missing from the text, or the form of the first word of the text is corrupt, or the entire sentence is unintelligible. In any case, "BeRESHIT" stands on its own within the sentence, as if it were absolute, to say "(i) in, with, by, near, etc., ... (ii) the or a (iii) first with respect to time, space, importance, logical order, narrative order, etc., ... (iv) of [blank!]," where the "blank" could be an implied term of reference that Be-RESHIT modifies. As the Hebrew is not clear, so the translation should be ambiguous. This is the sense in which I render it by the English idiom, "To begin with."

"ELOHIM" simply means "God." Note that whereas the term "YHVH" (which does not occur in our text) is a proper name, "Elohim" is not. It is a general term that refers contextually to a single entity. The same can be said for almost all of the nouns mentioned. However, some of them are made definite by the suffix "H," while others are not. For example, while our text states "the sky" and "the earth," it also says "grass" and "deep."[4] "Elohim" is like the latter two terms, viz., it is "God" and not "the-God." Based on this lack of either a proper name or the use of the definite article in referring to the deity, a possible reading of our text is that the creator is an unidentified member of a class of entities called "God." However, the summary of the account of creation that immediately follows — Genesis 2:4-5 — explicitly associates ELOHIM with YHVH, to indicate that the deity of creation is not just a god, but the deity called "YHVH," in order to affirm that the creator is the deity whom human history recognizes as the god of Abraham, Isaac and Jacob.

---

[4] Most of the nouns in our text appear only in the singular form, sometimes with and sometimes without a definite article. However, there are exceptions. Celestial lights, seas, signs, appointed seasons, and years appear in the plural. Dry land, sun, moon and the so-called sea-serpents appear only with a definite article. Finally, creepers, deep, evening and morning, fruit, God's wind, herb and grass, place, seas, TOHU and BOHU, work, signs, appointed seasons, and years appear only without a definite article.

"BARA" is a verb which always is translated as "creates." However, whatever it does mean, it does not literally mean "creates." Our primary use of the English term, "to create" is as a direct action verb with which we associate what artists or craftspeople do as agents to objects like stones or pieces of cloth or paper in order to produce certain artificial products like statues, paintings, or poems. However, there are perfectly good Hebrew terms to express this usage, viz., "YATZAR," or even "'ASAH" (more literally, "to do"), but not "BARA."[5]

The verb "BARA" is a simple, active construction (what is called a "kal") in the third person, singular form of the perfect tense. The verb is used in this form four times in Genesis,[6] once more in the Pentateuch,[7] and six more times in the Hebrew Scriptures.[8] The simple, active construction of the verb appears in other forms 23 times[9] in the Bible. In every one of these cases the agent of the action is God. The object or product (as the case may be) of God's distinctive action in every instance but one[10] is either the universe or human beings, and in most cases God's act describes or alludes to or parallels what is described in this first chapter of Genesis. In other words, the term "BARA" functions

---

[5] This is not to claim that BARA has no association whatsoever with creating. On the contrary, there is every reason to believe that there is a connection between what God does when he BARAs and what He does when he creates. For example, Amos 4:13 draws a parallel between God BARAing the wind (RUACH) and creating (YATZAR) the mountains. Rather, the point is for God to BARA does mean that God creates, and that while BARA may be in some sense similar to what God does when He creates, it is not like what anyone else does when they create. The same point applies to God "doing" something. For example, Isa 45:12 draws a parallel between God BARAing ADAM and making ('ASAH) the earth.

[6] Gen 1:1, 27; 2:3 and 5:2.

[7] Dt 4:32.

[8] Isa 4:5; 40:26; 41:20; 45:18; Jer 31:22; and Mal 2:10.

[9] Gen 1:21, 27; 5:1; 6:7; Nu 16:30; Isa 40:28; 42:5; 43:1, 7, 15; 45:7, 8, 12, 18; 54:16; 57:19; 65: 17, 18; Amos 4:13; Ps 51:12; 89:13, 48; and Eccl 12:1.

[10] Viz., in Gen 1:21 (to be discussed below) where the objects of God's action are the various forms of entities that reside in the seas.

primarily to express the unique act, whatever it is, that God does here to or with the universe and humanity.[11]

Hebrew verbs appear in seven different constructions. Grammar books list them as (1) the simple active, (2) the simple passive, (3) the intensive active, (4) the intensive passive, (5) the causative active, (6) the causative passive, and (7) the reflective. The names suggest that the root verb is the same in every construction, except for the way it is used. However, more often than not, root verbs in different constructions have very different meanings that cannot be explained simply by saying one form is active or passive, intensive and/or causative and/or reflective or not. This is the case with the verb in question. Its root consonants are bet (ב), resh (ר), and aleph (א). Besides its use in the simple active construction, it also appears in the Hebrew Scriptures as the intensive active (what is called "piel") four times. In one case, the actor cuts people with a sword;[12] in two cases he cuts down trees with an axe;[13] in one case he makes a sign-post,[14] which presumably involves carving wood with a knife. What is common to all of these examples is that someone cuts something with something else. Hence, the verb expresses a three term relation in which an acting agent changes the nature of a recipient object by means of using some kind of tool.

This root-form also occurs thirteen times[15] as BaRIY [i.e., as bet (ב), resh (ר), yod (י), aleph (א)]. In these cases the term expresses something being fat and/or healthy. Because the root means "to cut" in the intensive active, and "to be fat and/or healthy" in a non-verbal form, does not mean that "BARA" means "God cuts something (a) with something (b) to make something (c) that is fat and healthy." Still all of these forms share a common root, which *prima facie* suggests that, whatever it is that God does at first, it has some connotations of cutting

---

[11] HA-ADAM and, by implication, the BeNAI ADAM. BeNAI ADAM, who are not referred to explicitly in our text, are human beings. HA-ADAM, as we shall see below, really is not humanity. It is "the human."
[12] Ez 23:47.
[13] Josh 17:15 and 18.
[14] Ez 21:24.
[15] Gen 41:2, 4, 5, 7, 18, 20; Jud 3:17; 1 Kgs 5:3; Ez 34:3; Hab 1:16; Zech 11:16; Ps 73:4 and Dan 1:15.

and being fat/healthy. However, whatever those connotations are, they need not have any association with time.

In modern Hebrew the tense of a verb expresses time. The perfect tense is used for the past, the imperfect for the future, and the active participle for the present. However, as a general rule, the form of verbs does not itself express time in biblical Hebrew. This role tends syntactically to be the function of adverbs. The tense of the verb itself tends instead to express the state of the action asserted, viz., whether or not it is complete. Hence, "BARA" asserts some sort of completed action directly performed by God, irrespective of any temporal reference for the action. Furthermore, that action may express a three term relationship in which God uses some thing(s) as a means to affect some other thing(s) for the latter's well-being.

How then should this critical term be translated? The choice is somewhat arbitrary, since no English verb adequately expresses what it should stipulate here, viz., an action uniquely characteristic of a deity. The term encompasses everything that God does to the planet earth and the sky. At this general level, telling (YOMER) functions as a general synonym of BARA, since everything comes to be by God telling it to be. At the same time this one general act is expressed as three distinct kinds of actions through three separate verbs. One, telling (YOMER) some things to bring forth other things, viz., earth to bring forth vegetation[16] and land life,[17] and water to bring forth sea life.[18] Two, naming (YIKRA) things, viz., day and night,[19] sky,[20] earth and seas.[21] Three, making ('ASAH) things, viz., a (so-called) firmament,[22] the sun and the moon,[23] things that live on the planet earth,[24] and the human being.[25] Given the long historical association of the verb BARA with human creativity, it

---

[16] Gen 1:11.
[17] Gen 1:24.
[18] Gen 1:20.
[19] Gen 1:5.
[20] Gen 1:8.
[21] Gen 1:10.
[22] Gen 1:7.
[23] Gen 1:16.
[24] Gen 1:25.
[25] Gen 1:26.

would be least misleading to avoid the otherwise acceptable English term, "creates." Better choices would be "produces" or "brings into being," because they are more ambiguous than "creates." Even better would "declares to be," since it highlights the text's emphasis on God's act as a kind of speech. The best choices are either to use the Hebrew term itself as an English verb or to make the noun, "God" into a verb, i.e., to translate either "God baras" or "God gods." Of the two, I prefer the latter. Making "god" a verb has the advantage of indicating that there is some form of identity between what God does to the universe and what God is. It also helps convey the sense that the verb that expresses God's act is independent of any time frame.

"ET Ha-SHAMAYIM Ve-ET HA-ARETZ" is the product of God's act. In general, what is produced is the universe. "ET ... Ve-ET" tells us that the associated terms are the direct object of the verb. Hence, verse 1 asserts that the universe is primarily divisible into two units — one called the SHAMAYIM, and the other called the ERETZ.

"HA-SHAMAYIM" could be the sky or heaven. Within the framework of our text, as well as within the entire Pentateuch, "heaven" is not a good translation. There is nothing within Genesis, or within most of the books of the Hebrew Scriptures for that matter, to suggest that its author(s) made a radical, qualitative, ontological separation in the universe between what is material and what is spiritual.[26] Furthermore, we are told below that the term names what divides the water into two distinct regions,[27] and that it is the space occupied by the sun, the moon, and the other astronomical bodies.[28] Hence, "sky" is the best translation.

---

[26] For example, it is unlikely that when the Bible speaks of a messenger of God (MALAKH) it designates what we have come to mean by an "angel," viz., a spiritual entity, qualitatively different from a human being. A more likely view would be that these divine messengers are just that, messengers, whose nature is not specified in the biblical text other than to say what they are not, viz., they are not fish, birds, or animals, who somehow are different kinds of entities than humans. It is significant to note that they are not listed among the objects that God produces.

[27] Gen 1:8.

[28] Gen 1:14-16.

"HA-ARETZ" is the earth. The term "earth" could designate an element,[29] a kind of material,[30] and/or a region of space. We shall see below that the term functions in all three ways within our text. However, in this verse, because it stands in opposition to SHAMAYIM, clearly the term "earth" refers to the planet, viz., the region of space that includes what is not in the sky, notably, vegetation and animals.

It is important to recognize that there is no sky until verse 8, and there is no planet earth until verse 19. Hence, no coherent reading of this verse could claim that it asserts that the first thing God produces is the sky and the earth. A better reading would be to separate this first verse from the rest of the narrative as a topic title. In other words, what the first verse says is that the subject matter of this text is an account of how God produces the sky and the earth.

Genesis 1:2

והארץ היתה תהו ובהו
VeHA-ARETZ HAYeTAH TOHU VAVOHU
The (space of) earth is devoid of value,

"Ve" normally is translated "and," but not always. As the text was written there was no punctuation. Within this framework, "Ve" functions to indicate what constitutes a distinct thought unit from what preceded. Whether the units marked off in this way should be separated by periods, commas, colons, or semi-colons depends on what the content of the consecutive units are and how they are logically related. In many contexts (including this one), it functions to begin a new sentence, and, as such, it requires no translation into English.

"HA-ARETZ" is either the element earth or the planet earth. At this initial stage, there is no sky. Hence, the element earth is a more likely interpretation. If the term names the planet, then it names the space that the planet will occupy, since nothing that the earth contains has yet been produced. Hence, following the latter line of interpretation, a more adequate translation would be "the space that is intended to be occupied by the planet earth." To render the term in this

---

[29] Viz., earth as opposed to, for example, fire, air or water.
[30] Viz., the land mass of the planet as opposed to the seas.

way makes its meaning more like the term, "sky," as it should be, i.e., as a space to be occupied rather than an occupied space. The two interpretations can be combined as "the space of earth," where the term "earth" means the element.

"HAYeTAH" is the perfect tense of the verb, "to be." It indicates that the state of the space reserved for the planet earth is stable, i.e., it is the way it is described; it is not becoming that way.

"TOHU VAVOHU" are often translated as "null and void." The expression is intended to describe the way that the earth is before God does anything to it. "VOHU" (or, "BOHU") occurs only three times in all of the Hebrew Scriptures.[31] In every case it appears together with TOHU. Jeremiah uses the two terms in conjunction precisely as they are used here in Genesis, viz., to assert the state of the space of the earth before God does anything to it. In Isaiah's case, the usage is somewhat different, but only slightly more enlightening. The context of their use is insufficient to show what they mean. However, the two terms are not conjoined within the Isaiah text, but they appear in such a way as to indicate that they are synonyms. Hence, the meaning of "VOHU" rests upon the meaning of TOHU.

"TOHU" makes sixteen solo appearances within the Hebrew Scriptures.[32] Of particular interest is its function in the the fortieth chapter of Isaiah. Verse 17 asserts that God considers all of the nations to be TOHU, which is described as being like "AYIN" (אין) and an instance of "EFES" (אפס).[33] Both AYIN and EFES express something that is negative. That number which is the lack of any number, viz., zero, is EFES. Similarly, a grammatically affirmative sentence is made negative by the insertion of AYIN. Both words do something, but the something they do is negative. Consequently, TOHU, and its synonym BOHU, also seem to have a negative valuative function. In the Isaiah case, the value assigned to the nations of the world and their rulers, viz., TOHU, is a no-value, i.e., a value that is nothing positive. Similarly, in Deuteronomy 32:10,[34] a wilderness (MIDBAR) is called a land that is

---

[31] Gen 1:2; Jer 4:23 and Isa 34:11.

[32] Dt 32:10; 1 Sam 12:21; Isa 24:10; 29:21; 40:17, 23; 41:29; 44:9; 45:18-19; 49:4 and 59:4; Job 6:18; 12:24; 26:7 and Ps 107:40.

[33] Similarly, in verse 23 their rulers are called both TOHU and AYIN.

[34] The only other occurrence of the term in the Pentateuch.

TOHU, i.e., a land that has a lack. What it lacks is what makes any land not a wilderness, viz., vegetation. In other words, all land has a certain amount of vegetation, and that amount in the case of a wilderness is zero, i.e., TOHU. Hence, what it means to say here in Genesis that the space of earth is TOHU and BOHU is that this space and/or its elementary occupant have a negative value, which means that the affirmed value of the space that is the origin of the universe is zero, i.e., nothing at all.

וחשך על-פני תהום
VeCHOSHEKH 'AL-PeNAI TeHOM
with dark at (every dimension of its) depth,

"CHOSHEKH" is dark. Like being devoid of value, being dark is something, but the something that it is is negative. In fact, Ecclesiastes 6:4 associates it with HEVEL (הבל), whose most literal sense is, being worthless.[35]

It is important to note that this dark, like the earth and its non-value, is something substantive that is already present at the origin of the universe. The same can be said for the so-called deep and the wind of God. It is true that Isaiah affirms that God created dark,[36] and similar statements can be found for these other entities as well. However, there is no statement in our text that God produces them. In fact, given that the primary subject matter of Genesis 1 is an account of the origin of the universe and its inhabitants, this omission is *prima facie* evidence that their existence precedes the universe that God produces.

"'AL-PeNAI" affirms some kind of relationship between the dark and the so-called deep. What that relationship is depends on what is being related. "'AL" is a preposition that has the association[37] of something being above something else. "PeNAI" is the construct form of "PANIM." "PANIM" is the same in both the singular and the plural. It

---

[35] The context of its occurrence in Ecclesiastes has to do with miscarriage, where the dead fetus is described as something that comes in HEVEL and departs in CHOSHEKH, i.e., it is worthless both when it enters into and departs from the world.

[36] Isa 45:7.

[37] By analogy with the verb, "rises" ('ALAH) (עלה).

means a face, and, by extension, it can also mean the front of something — its exterior and/or its surface — i.e., that part of something that is immediately present to something else. It is this sense of "presence" that is most common to all of its different uses. Hence, a PANIM can be the way something appears or looks. In this context, the expression, "'AL-PeNAI" means that dark and the so-called deep are immediately present to each other. If dark and deep are spatial objects, then the preposition "'AL-PeNAI" would suggest that the dark is immediately above, i.e., on top of, the deep. If they are not, then the expression must have a different meaning. For example, if the context deals with a linear ordering of objects, then the assertion that one thing is 'AL PeNAI another means that the former appears in the ordering immediately before the latter.

"TeHOM" usually is translated as "deep." In general, this term is associated with the notion of depth. As such, it could mean the empty dimensions of the space of the earth, i.e., its length, width, and depth, and (possibly) its time as well. On this interpretation, the earth's depth is an uncreated something that is negative — like the dark and (possibly) the TOHU and BOHU as well. In this case what the affirmed relation between dark and depth would be is one of mutual entailment, viz., what is dark and what has dimension are conjoined throughout the empty space of the element, earth. In other words, the expression asserts that this space that is empty of anything positive still is something, viz., a consistently dark depth.

A different interpretation of this phrase occurs once it is set within the larger framework of the entire Hebrew Scriptures, where the term, "TeHOM" generally functions to name the division of the waters set immediately below the planet earth. In this case the affirmed relation between dark and deep would be one of spatial location. It would say that the dark, empty[38] space of the earth is located immediately above the region of water.

As long as our focus is solely on the Genesis account of creation, the former interpretation of "TeHOM" is more likely. On the first interpretation, depth ontologically parallels dark as a negative characterization of the substance of the original space of earth. Furthermore, on the second interpretation, TeHOM would constitute a

---

[38] I.e., empty of anything positive.

third division of space, distinct from both earth and sky. Certainly such an interpretation is consistent with other sections of the Pentateuch.[39] However, as we have already seen, the Genesis account of the origin of the universe asserts a two-way, not a three-way, basic division of space into earth and sky.

It is possible to reconcile these two interpretations. It could be the case that the term "TeHOM" functions in both ways. It should be remembered that at this stage of our narrative there is no sky, and the earth is not as yet anything at all. It makes little sense here to say that a nothing is spatially above anything at all. At the same time, the next phrase in this verse makes the first mention of the water, which, while uncreated, is something positive. Hence, it can be said that our text asserts a strong association between deep and dark at the origin that will become a strong association between deep and water at the end. At first, the region of elementary earth is dark throughout its dimensions, i.e., is dark everywhere. Subsequently it will receive light into its domain. At the end, only the region of the waters below the earth will remain thoroughly dark.[40]

ורוח אלהים מרחפת על־פניהמים:
VeRUACH ELOHIM MeRACHEFET 'AL-PeNAI HA-MAYIM.
while God's wind (wisdom) hovers at the water.

"RUACH" most often is translated as "spirit." However, this translation is not correct. The English term "spirit," like the terms

---

[39] For example, Ex 20:4 and Dt 5:8.

[40] Historians of the biblical period commonly draw attention to the linguistic similarity between the term "TeHOM" and the name of the Mesopotamian female diety, Tiamat, whom ancient Near Eastern cosmogonies associate with the seas, and personify as a sea-serpent or dragon. Undoubtedly, this analogy is appropriate. However, within our text, TeHOM has no personal characteristics. Whatever were its associations with deity, it has lost them in our text. In this respect it is important to note that in the next phrase it is wind, not TeHOM, that is associated with deity and water. Our TeHOM has no stipulated relationship with deity and is associated with the dark of the earth. Furthermore, the so-called sea-serpents (TeNINIM) are not produced until the sixth day, their origin is attributed to the waters, and TeHOM plays no role in their generation.

"heaven" and "angel," presupposes a radical dualism of the spiritual and the material that does not fit the ontology of the Hebrew Scriptures. "Wind" is less misleading. However, the wind in this case is not just wind; it is "RUACH ELOHIM," viz., God's wind.

"RUACH ELOHIM" is not God, and, like the other objects already listed (viz., earth, dark, and depth), it is not something that God produces. At the same time, this wind is unique among the original things in two ways. First, it is not mentioned again in our narrative. Second, it is something that belongs to God. Hence, "RUACH" need not be the general term for wind. It could be a special wind, viz., God's wind.

The use of this expression within our text suggests two possible interpretations. First, if we situate Genesis 1 within the corpus of the Hebrew Scriptures, "RUACH ELOHIM" could mean divine wisdom. This interpretation is explicitly affirmed in Proverbs. In verse 8:22, wisdom (CHAKHMAH) says that "the Lord took possession of me (KANANIY)" as "the first of His way (RESHIT DARKO)," which is explained as "His ancient product (MIF'ALAV MEOZ)" that is "prior (KEDEM)" to anything else. The next verse reiterates the statement. Here wisdom says that she was set up "from eternity (ME'OLAM)," which is interpreted at the end of the verse to mean "at first (MEROSH), before (MIKADMAI) earth." The allusion of "RESHIT DARKO" (the first of His way) to "BeRESHIT" in Genesis 1:1 is obvious. The author(s) of Proverbs are asserting that "BeRESHIT BARA ELOHIM" means that God used his first principle, viz., wisdom, to create the universe. Genesis 1:2 gives a name, viz., the divine wind, to what Genesis 1:1 simply calls a first principle.

Second, if we locate our text within the corpus of cosmogonies found in the classical Mediterranean world, the expression could mean a composite of the elements air and fire. The most direct parallel is the account of the origin of the universe by the Stoic, Zeno of Cition.[41]

---

[41] Lived 332-262 B.C.E. on Cyprus. It is no less reasonable to assume a common cultural matrix for all Mediterranean thought, classical Greek as well as ancient Near Eastern, than it is to use one book in the Hebrew Scriptures to interpret another. Most biblical critics locate our text in the Babylonian Exile as a product of the impact of Babylonian culture on the Jewish people during the 6th century B.C.E. From this perspective, it is reasonable to look at the entire corpus of Greek science for parallels, since classical Greek scholars affirm that the milieu of ancient science extends beyond the Greek city states through the eastern borders of

Based on the standard cosmogonies of the classical Mediterranean world that we know from the pre-Socratic philosophers, we can anticipate that the Bible's cosmogony will include the standard four elements — fire, air, water, and earth. Our text explicitly includes water and earth, but no direct mention is made of fire and air. Wind is an obvious candidate for that function.

Zeno of Cition, in particular, presents the following picture of the early universe.

	Element	Quality	Causal Effect
Active	fire	hot	Physical Activity
	air	cold	Biological Activity
Passive	Earth	dry	
	water	moist	

The basic materials of the universe are divided into active and passive elements. The passive ones are earth and water. Their primary qualities, respectively, are dry and moist. The active elements are fire and air. The primary quality of fire is hot, in virtue of which fire causes physical activity. Similarly, the primary quality of air is cold, in virtue of which air causes biological activity. PNEUMA, like RUACH, basically means wind, breath, or spirit. Zeno tells us that it is a mixture of the two active elements, fire and air. Its function is to bind the passive elements, water and earth, into the physical substances that occupy the entire universe. Hence, on this interpretation, God's wind is the active, positive element that God will use to transform the passive, negative elements of earth and water into the actual deep space of our present universe.

"HA-MAYIM" is the water. Like "HA-ARETZ," this term names an element and/or the original space of the element. The noun is the same in both the singular (water) and plural (waters). However, as the text will subsequently make clear, at this stage of development the space of the element water is undifferentiated into subregions. Hence, it

---

the Mediterranean Sea into the Babylonian/Persian empire. At least one of Zeno's predecessors, viz., Thales of Milos, predates the authorship of our text, and many of the classic natural philosopher-scientists who influenced Zeno were contemporary with the Babylonian Exile, viz., the Miletians Anaximander and Anaximenes, as well as Heracleitus and Pythagoras.

would not make any sense to speak here of "waters" rather than "water."

The phrase, "VeRUACH ELOHIM MeRACHEFET 'AL-PeNAI HA-MAYIM" affirms a close association between the water and God's wind, in contrast to the dark that is related to the depth. As dark is a negative entity, God's wind is a positive entity. Similarly, as depth has a negative sense in characterizing a kind of space, so the term "MAYIM" has a positive sense. "The water" is intended to be both the positive element, water, and the space occupied by this second element. Furthermore, like the element earth and its space, the water is not a product of God's action. However, there is a difference. Whereas the earth is devoid of value, the water, in virtue of being linked to God's wind, is not value free.

"MeRACHEFET Al-PeNAI" expresses the link between God's wind and the water. The verb[42] appears only three times in all of the Hebrew Scriptures. Jeremiah uses it[43] in the simple, active construction to describe his despondency over the moral corruption of his society. Specifically he says that as his heart (LIBIY) is broken (NISHBAR), so his bones shake or quiver (RACHAFU). In our text the verb appears in an intensive active construction. Its only other use in this form is in Deuteronomy 32:11, where it describes a mother eagle hovering (YeRACHEF) in the air over her young. The sense of the verb in Deuteronomy directly parallels its use here. The eagle is standing still, i.e., there is no change of place, but it is not at rest, i.e., it is active. If the bird did nothing at all, the air currents would carry the eagle away from its location. Rather, it must be in constant motion, viz., its wings shaking or quivering, in order to remain motionless. Similarly in our text, for the spatial relationship between God's wind and the water to remain constant (i.e., unchanging, as if nothing were happening at all), the wind must be constantly active.

In summary, this second verse of the Genesis account of God's production of the universe, which is the first verse of the actual narrative, succinctly describes the zero point of origin of the universe that is the material given to God to construct humanity's material world. It says that the space of the passive element, earth, is devoid of

---

[42] Whose root is resh (ר), chet (ח), and pe (פ).
[43] Jer 23:9.

value, with dark throughout its depth, while God's active, principle element of wind remains in a constant state of agitation throughout the space of the passive element, water. We may visualize this verbal picture as follows:

It is a picture of pure space that, while it contains nothing, is itself something. The space is differentiated into two regions, each with its own inherent, distinct qualities. One is a passive, thoroughly negative earth; the other is a water made active (and therefore imbued with some value) by a divine principle of activity called wind. The text implies an ontology of opposites to be integrated through divine action. The dualities are passive-active, negative-positive, nonvalue-value, and earth-water. All of them constitute a general space that can, but does not yet, have value. The following account of creation is a narrative of God giving this stuff value. Just what "value" means within our text remains to be seen.

DAY 1

Genesis 1:3

ויאמר אלהים יהי אור ויהי אור:
VA-YOMER ELOHIM YeHIY OR VA-YeHIY OR
God says, "Let there be a light," and light comes to be.

"VA-YOMER ELOHIM" expresses God's first act upon the primordial space of the universe. It is a speech act. "YOMER" means, "says."

What God says is, "YeHIY OR." The first "YeHIY" functions as a singular, masculine jussive of the verb, to be. He says, "let there be!"

The commanding is immediately followed by the happening. There is a conjunction between God ordering light and light coming to be. The second "YeHIY," i.e., the verb in the phrase, "VA-YEHIY OR," has the shortened form of "YIHYEH" — the third person, singular in the imperfect tense of the simple, active conjugation of the verb, to be. However, when YeHIY is combined with the consonant of conjunction, VA-, the verb functions as if its tense were perfect.[1] I interpret the imperfect tense of the verb to indicate that the verb expresses that the subject's state of being is dynamic, i.e., in flux, in contrast to the perfect tense, which I take to mean that the verb expresses the subject's state is

---

[1] The grammatical rule of biblical Hebrew in this case is called "the Waw Consecutive." A verb attached to the conjunction, VA (or, Waw), whose form is imperfect, functions as if its form is perfect. Similarly, a verb attached to the conjunction, VA, whose form is perfect, functions as if its form is imperfect.

stable, i.e., constant or at rest. Furthermore, I interpret the use of form of the imperfect tense of a verb whose meaning is rendered by the consonant of the conjunction to function as if it were in the perfect tense to mean that what acts in a dynamic state does so towards an end, the achievement of which renders it stable. In other words, the act of being expressed here by the verb, to be, is a movement towards an end. The state of the produced light is the stable end of what is to be understood as a dynamic, end-directed activity. Hence, "becomes" or "comes to be" as an English translation of this verb is preferable to "is" or "there is."

What God orders there to be is "OR." "OR" usually means light. However, this "light" cannot be what we ordinarily mean by this word. For the same reasons that the term "creates" is misleading, so the term "light" is misleading. The phenomena that we normally associate with "light" are emissions in the form of rays from certain kinds of bodies — most notably, from the sun and other stars — that modern scientists describe in terms of an electromagnetic radiation product of the thermal motion of the molecular constituents of these bodies. However, the term "OR" in our text names an object, not a phenomena, whose existence is independent of any other kind of body. It certainly is not the light of the sun or the stars, since these objects do not exist until the conclusion of the fourth day.[2]

The author(s) of Psalm 104 characterizes this light as something analogous to a garment (SAMLAH) that God wears as a robe.[3] Some statements in the midrash call it a special kind of element that is intended for the World-To-Come that is not part of our material universe. These most ancient Jewish commentaries on the text share in common the judgment that this light is something radically different from anything found in our present physical universe. In contrast, Ibn Ezra says it is the material element, fire, while several other medieval biblical

---

[2] The medieval commentator, Gersonides, rejects this interpretation. He claims that the term functions within our text with four different levels of meaning — viz., as (1) perceptible light, and, by extension, (2) clear sight, (3) (Aristotelian) form, and/or (4) the adequate cognition of the separate intellects — but that the primary sense of the term is the light that we associate with sunlight.

[3] Psalm 104:1-2. "... Oh YHVH my ELOHIM, ... You wear glory and splendor. (You are someone) who wraps himself with OR like a garment ... ."

commentators[4] identify it with a fifth celestial element from which astronomical bodies are constructed. However, these medieval interpretations exceed any explicit evidence present in the words of our text.

This light is best understood in connection with its opposite, dark. Both are things that in every significant respect are opposites. As dark is a nothing, i.e., a negative entity, that is not a divine product, so light is a something, i.e., a positive entity, that God produces. Whatever this dark is, it is different from, but none the less somehow associated with, the darkness of our universe. Similarly, whatever this light is, it is different from, but none the less somehow associated with, the light of our universe. However, what else this pair may be cannot be explained solely on the basis of our text.

In summary, God's first act is to order light to be-come. This light is the opposite of the primordial dark. At first there is a passive, negative dark that pervades space. It also is unintelligible, because there is nothing else with which to contrast it. Now God makes the dark something distinct by generating an active, positive light. This event is God's first act of separation within the initially given space of our universe.

Genesis 1:4

וירא אלהים את־האור כי טוב

VA-YAR ELOHIM ET-HA-OR KI TOV

God perceives that the light is excellent,

"VA-YAR" expresses what *prima facie* is God's second act. "YAR" usually means "sees." First, God says something that, in virtue of his saying, happens. Then God sees what happens.

"YAR" is the shortened form of the third person, singular of the verb, RA-AH (הר) in the imperfect tense of the simple, active conjugation. Because the verb is consecutive with the consonant of conjunction (VA-) its sense is that of the perfect tense. It need not mean "sees" in the sense of having a visual sensation. The term can equally well be translated as "perceives," "understands," "conceives," or even, "feels." Which English term is preferable largely depends on factors

---

[4] Viz., Rashi, Nachmanides and Sforno.

external to our text, most notably, whether or not God has a body or anything like a body. "YAR" can mean "sees" in a literal sense only if it is intelligible in some literal sense to say that God has eyes. If he does not, then "sees" is not correct, and any of these other, equally literal, English translations is preferable. For example, Ibn Ezra takes the verb to mean that God sees in thought, i.e., he understands or conceives. His interpretation is perfectly intelligible in English as well. It is in this sense that we use the verb, to see, when we say, "I see what you mean," meaning, I understand what you are saying.

"KI" introduces what God sees. What he sees is a sentence, viz., that the light is good. In other words, this verse asserts that God understands something about the light that he produced, viz., that it is good. Hence, "conceives" is a better translation in this context than sees, since sentences are the kinds of things that are understood rather than seen. However, both of these terms — conceives and understands — are too precise for this context. Usually any use of this verb will have visual connotations. Even when it means understanding, the choice implies that visual sensation has some connection with the conception. Hence, in this context, where it is desirable not to prejudge what the text says about God's nature, "perceives" is a better translation. "Perceives" has the virtue of being less clear than "understands" and "conceives" precisely because "perceives" alludes to sensation. Similarly, it is less misleading than "sees" as a translation, because "perceives" is more common in a non-sensual use than is "sees."

What God perceives is that the light is "TOV." "TOV" is one of the most important technical terms in our text. Like the word, "YOM" (day), it occurs seven times, and, as such, it functions as one of the ways that God's act of producing the universe is subdivided.[5] The usual translation of "TOV" is "good." As such it is a positive value term. However, both the Hebrew and the English are equally equivocal as to the kind of value

---

[5] God perceives [1] the light (vs. 4), [2] the seas and dry land (vs. 10), [3] the earth's vegetation (vs. 12), [4] the star-filled sky (vs. 18), [5] the living inhabitants of the seas and the air (vs. 21), and [6] the land animals (vs. 25) to be good, and he perceives [7] everything he produced (vs. 31) to be "very" good.

judgment involved. Moral value is only one possibility.⁶ Having a "good name" (SHEM TOV) says something about a person's reputation, but not his character. Similarly, being "good looking" (TOV MAREH) is morally neutral. The same is true of a gem, which in Hebrew is called a "good stone" (EVEN TOVAH). In general, the term "TOV," like its Greek counterpart, ARETE, is associated with a positive value judgment of a task performed. In this sense, the term has more to do with virtues that may, but need not, have moral connotations. For example, a "good thief" is a very skilled thief, who, in virtue of his skill, is morally less desirable than a "bad thief." In other words, "TOV" is a term that equivocally expresses excellence of all kinds. Whether or not the sense of excellence involved in God's judgment of his products is moral is not specified in our text.

Since the verb is in an imperfect form in the Waw Consecutive, the term "YAR" suggests that God's judgment expresses a limit function, i.e., the stable achievement of what is essentially a purposive, dynamic action. In other words, whatever is the virtue of the light, the judgment is as dynamic as the light itself. However, this is not to say that the dynamic has a time frame. We have already seen that verbs in biblical Hebrew are atemporal. Just as God's act of saying is not distinct from his producing what he says, so his judgment of the value of his action need not be understood to be distinct. This is one of many examples in our text where what is a single event appears in linguistic expression to be multiple acts.

ויבדל אלהים בין האור ובין החשך:
VA-YAVDEL ELOHIM BAYN HA-OR UVAYN HA-CHOSHEKH
and God separates the light from the dark.

---

⁶ Rashi takes the term to mean that this specific act of production is complete. Ibn Ezra says that the term declares that everything that occurs before its stipulation is a single unit. Nachmanides thinks the term has to do with the enduring quality of the product, viz., that it will persist forever. Only Sforno interprets the term in a moral sense. According to him, that God perceives something to be good means that he desires it to be a moral end that is expressible through knowledge of the universe as a whole.

This phrase makes explicit what is entailed by God producing light where there is only dark (verse 3), viz., that light and dark are different things. "YAVDEL" is a third person, singular form in the imperfect in the Waw Consecutive of the active, causative conjugation of the verb, "to separate." It makes clear the kind of act God performs, viz., an act that causes a separation. However, this separating is no more distinct from God's act of saying than are his acts of producing and judging. As what God says, in the very saying itself, happens, so what God does, in the very doing, is judged to be good. Similarly, producing light where there is dark is no different than separating light and dark. As when what is pure is mixed with what is impure, the compound is consistently impure, so, when light is mixed with dark, there is only dark.

As the compound sentence, "John Wilkes Booth fired his gun, shot Abraham Lincoln, killed him, and murdered the President" expresses four different aspects of a single action, so what God says, produces, esteems, and distinguishes are a single act. It is the nature of the way a story is told that what it describes seems *prima facie* to occur serially, and, therefore, in time. However, this temporal consequence arises solely from the inescapably linear nature of narrative language; it need not be true of what the language describes. At first there is dark, and by ordering light into existence, the dark becomes distinguishable as not being the light. It is this separating aspect of God's act that he judges to be excellent.

The question arises, since the separation of light and dark entails that they are not together, where are they situated in relationship to each other? Verse two suggests that it is the space of the earth that is dark. Hence, it could be the space of the water that becomes light. Conversely, if the narrative of our text parallels Zeno's cosmogony, it would be reasonable to associate the light with the elementary fire that is a component of God's wind. In this case the wind hovering over the water would expand beyond the water's external surface to form an outer shell of enlightened elementary air that our text identifies as light. In this case, the space of the universe would be pictured as follows:

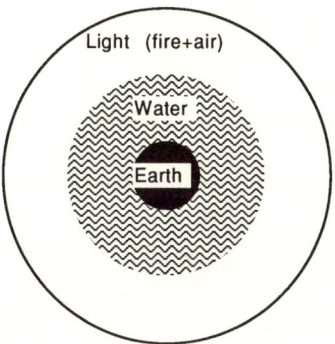

However, it also is possible that the domains of light and dark are both distinct areas of space, either independent of the regions of water and earth or situated within the earth's space. The domain of dark could be dotted with multiple regions of light, or the combined area could be divided into two distinct semi-circular regions, one dark and the other light. Given this last option, the light could be above, below, or alongside of the dark. As we shall see, the next verse of our text suggests an answer to this question.

In summary, verse 4 spells out a consequence of the divine act asserted in verse 3. God's ordering that light come to be entails an as-yet-unspecified separation that makes both the light and the dark distinct. Furthermore, this generative act of drawing distinctions is something that God judges to have a form of positive value.

<u>Genesis 1:5</u>

ויקרא אלהים לאור יום ולחשך קרא לילה
VA-YIKRA ELOHIM LA-OR YOM Ve-LA-CHOSHEKH KARA LAYLAH
God names the light "day" and the dark "night,"

"<u>YIKRA</u>" is a third person, singular, simple active conjugation in the imperfect tense in the Waw Consecutive of a verb whose root is kuf (ק), resh (ר), aleph (א). In this construction it means "calls," "proclaims," "reads," "recites," "summons," "assembles," and/or "names." It may also mean "happens" or "occurs." *Prima facie* this verb describes God's second action. What he first calls or commands to be now is proclaimed or summoned to have a name, in virtue of which it happens or occurs. However, the "naming" ought to be understood as a constituent part of the single act of divine production of the light in relation to the dark. The naming goes together with the saying and the separating. What God says is, but until what is is named as something distinct from something else named, the product is not anything at all, and, as such, cannot happen.

There is a sense in which what is said to become is not non-existent. However, it is not real until it is named as something distinct. Saying makes it be and naming makes it happen. Merely being/becoming is not happening/occuring; happening/occuring is being/becoming something definite, i.e., something definable, i.e., something that has a name.

The connotations of the verbs, saying and naming, are legal as well as ontological. Something that has no legal designation or classification has no status within a legal system. Until named, it stands outside the universe of the law. So here something not yet named is not part of the physical universe. In both cases, what is not named is, but, as it is, it is nothing at all. In the ontology of the Genesis creation narrative, there are negative things. They are things that are not yet something. The Hebrew Scriptures express this ontological duality as a distinction between things that do and do not have names.

The preposition "LA" stipulates the direct object of the action. The objects of the naming are the given dark and the produced light. The latter is proclaimed "day," and the former "night." There is dark independent of divine activity, but, as given, it is not anything at all. It is only with respect to the prior givenness of the dark that God's act of naming differs from his act of saying. Saying and naming together express producing something. The saying is producing, and the naming makes the product something. In the case of light, the two verbs combine to express a single production. However, as a given, dark need not be said. In this case, production consists solely in naming.

What links the saying and the naming is the separating. To say that something that is is something rather than nothing is to say what it is. To say what something is is to compare the subject to something else. On one hand, the something else must be sufficiently like the subject for comparison to be possible. On the other hand, they may not be identical. In other words, classification entails comparison, which emphasizes how things are the same, but comparison entails a real relationship of non-identity, which emphasizes how those same things are different. That two things can be classified in terms of each other means positively that they are related and negatively that they are not the same. In our text, dark becomes something only when God produces light. The light identifies the dark, and the dark identifies the light. It is their relation of opposition that establishes the reality of each as something. Hence, separation is itself an essential condition for production. What is is something when it is named; naming is classifying, and classifying expresses separation.

The light is proclaimed "YOM" and the dark is declared "LAYLAH." "<u>YOM</u>" means "day" and "<u>LAYLAH</u>" "night." These terms usually express the time period of the separate rotations of the sun and the planet earth relative to each other from a fixed point on the surface of the earth. The amount of time involved in that part of the rotations in which a designated area of the earth does not face the sun is called "night." "Day" either names the amount of time during which the designated earth area faces the sun, or, in a broader sense, it names the time of the complete cycle of alteration from day to night back to day, or from night to day back to night. It is during the period when they are not facing each other that the specified area is dark from lack of sunlight, and it is during the period when they face each other that the area is light with sunlight. Note that the primary referent of the terms "day" and "night" is the time period, and not the state of the specified earth surface during that time period.

The opposite is the case in our text, where "day" and "night" name the light and the dark respectively, independent of the sun, which does not come into existence until verse 16 on the fourth day. Furthermore, the terms "day" and "night" in our text directly name the objects, light and dark, without any reference to time.

What kinds of objects are the day and the night? At this stage of the narrative, they can only refer to the elementary space itself. In other words, the universal space in which water and earth are situated is divided into two regions, one filled with dark and the other with light. As the spatial region occupied by the element water is called "water" and the region occupied by the element earth is called "earth," so the region occupied by dark is called "night" and the region occupied by light is called "day." The entire space may be pictured as follows:

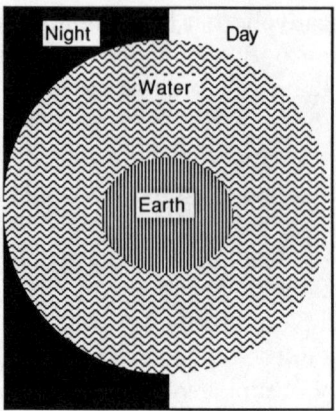

The spherical region of earth-space is surrounded by a ring of water-space. The combined space of earth and water are themselves situated within and penetrated by the space of a divine wind. This outer region may itself be a composite region of fire and air in which light and dark are now separated, i.e., made definite, into an area of the light, where fire dominates, and an area of dark, where air dominates.

It should be noted that our text says nothing about the dimensions of these regions of space. At this stage of the narrative's development, the earth core could be a sphere of zero radius, i.e., a mere geometric point. Similarly, our text is silent about their shape. In fact, some rabbinic philosophic commentators portray the space as spherical,[7] while

---

[7] For example, Sforno takes the term "HA-SHAMAYIM" (sky) in Gen 1:1 to designate the entire space of the universe. He argues that the first part of this term, SHAM (שם) , means "there," which indicates that "sky" designates a "distant place," i.e., a space. Furthermore, since the second part of the word, AYIM (ים), is a dual plural form, Sforno asserts that this space is divided into two equal dimensions. He identifies these dimensions to be the horizontal and the vertical. Based on this linguistic analysis, he concludes that space must be a sphere whose rotation is perfectly circular. The geometric picture behind his deduction is the following: From a single point draw two circles, one horizontal and the other vertical, that intersect each at right angles. Now add a second pair of circles from the same point from an infinitesimally different angle from the first pair. Sforno imagines a sphere to be composed of an

Day 1   35

some midrashic commentators picture space to be cubical.[8] A cubical view would be coherent with Plato's picture in the *Timaeus* of a universe

infinite number of such pairs of circles at different inclinations from each other. I.e.,

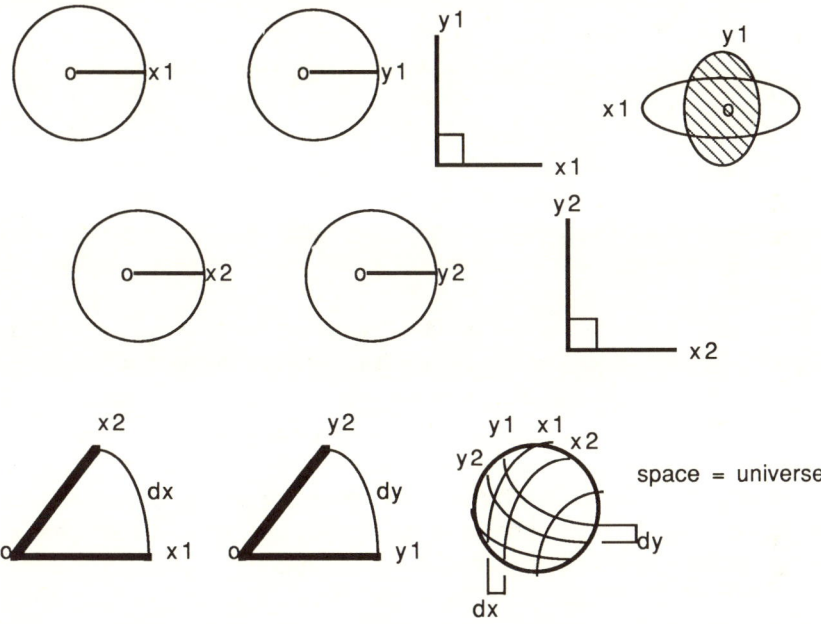

In other words, Sforno's deduction from his linguistic analysis of the term "sky" as spherical space presupposes, at an intuitive level, calculus, i.e., the complementary mathematical operations of differentiation and integration.

[8] In fact this alternate picture would be more coherent with many midrashic interpretations of creation. [For a general summary of early rabbinic cosmologies based on Genesis, see volume one of Louis Ginzberg's *The Legends of the Jews* (Philadelphia, The Jewish Publication Society of America, 1942).] Some of these texts discuss the dimensions of the different regions of space. A common picture places the space of the 'EVEN SHETIYAH [Literally, the "stone of slaughter." It is the stone for carrying out sacrifices within the Holy of Holies in the Temple. Purportedly this is the stone on which Abraham bound Isaac for

constructed from polygons, including cubes, that in turn are constructed from triangles. However, there is no other reason to prefer a cubical over a spherical interpretation of the spatial dimensions of the early universe. Again, there is nothing in the biblical text that can settle the matter one way or the other.

ויהי־ערב ויהי בקר יום אחד:
VA-YeHIY-'EREV VA-YeHIY BOKER YOM ECHAD
while evening and morning come to be one day.

"<u>EREV</u>" usually means "evening," viz., the time at which the sun sets, and "<u>BOKER</u>" usually means "morning" or "dawn," viz., when the sun makes its first appearance above the horizon. However, the usual meanings of these terms cannot be what they mean in our text for

---

sacrifice.] at the center of the universe, encompassed by the space of the Temple mount, which in turn is encompassed by the space of Jerusalem, the inhabited world, the uninhabited world, and finally a space further differentiated into the distinct regions of paradise and hell. Midrashic commentators make specific judgments about the magnitude of some of these regions. The unit of measurement is a "walking year," viz., the distance that a (presumably standard) man could walk in a single year. For example, the distances across the inhabited and the uninhabited regions of the earth are both 500 walking years. In every case a fixed point is taken from which the distance across the sphere is equal in length (viz., moving forward), width (viz., moving to the side), and height (viz., moving up). Presumably it is not possible from this point to move either down or back. In other words, the regions are pictured as a rectangle in which the point is a corner. That the distances from these corners are equal says that the rectangles are cubes, viz.,

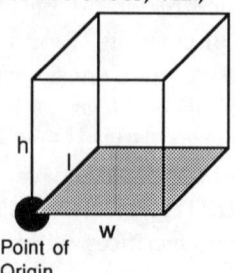

Point of Origin

precisely the same reasons that "YOM" and "LAYLAH" are not day and night. First, there does not as yet exist a sun. Second, there is nothing in our text to suggest any time reference.

Whatever they mean, they are existent entities related through a duality of opposites, i.e., they are contrary instances of the same kind of things. The root of the noun "BOKER" — bet (ב), kuf (ק), resh (ר) — offers no clue to the character of this relationship. The verb only appears in the intensive active conjugation in the Hebrew Scriptures where it means "to investigate" or "to critically examine" something. However, the root of the noun "'EREV" — ayin (ע), resh (ר), bet (ב) — is more enlightening. In the simple active conjugation it often means, "to be or to become dark," and, by extension, "to be or to become obscure." The sense of the verb as being/becoming obscure is related to its more frequent use in the intensive active conjugation as "to mix," and "to confuse." Hence, these verbal uses suggest that the noun has something to do with something being mixed or confused. In other words "evening" describes a state in which things become mixed and indistinguishable. Hence, "morning" should describe an opposite kind of state, viz., one in which these same kinds of things become clear and distinguishable. The things are light and dark. Consequently, "evening" refers to those places at which the outer semi-circle of light becomes increasing dark, where it is increasingly difficult to "see" anything, while "morning" refers to those places at which the outer semi-circle of dark becomes increasing light, where it is increasingly easy to "see" something. The combination of "evening and morning" means that there is no sharp line between the light of day and the dark of night; they fade into each other.

Sforno interpreted these two terms in the above way. In contrast, Ibn Ezra gave the terms a time frame. On his interpretation each day marks a complete rotation of the outer sphere of the universe itself, i.e., the days of Genesis are a measure of the time of the universe rather than the time of the earth. On his interpretation, evening and morning are those times, within the framework of universal time, when light and dark are mixed ('ERAV) so that they cannot be distinguished, i.e., they cannot be examined (BIKKER). In my opinion, Sforno's interpretation is closer to the general meaning of our text, for which no time frame is appropriate. In any case, the issue cannot be settled by the use of the terms "evening" and "morning" alone. Rather, how these terms are interpreted depends on how the term "day" functions throughout the narrative.

Our text divides God's production into seven days. The first differs from the others linguistically precisely because it is not called "first." Rather, it is said to be "one." The remaining seven days are all modified by ordinal numbers, i.e., they are called a second, third, fourth, fifth, sixth, and seventh day. However, the initial day is not called "first" (RISHON). Rather, it is modified by a cardinal number; it is said to be "<u>ECHAD</u>," i.e., "one." Whether or not this stylistic inconsistency was intentional is not self-evident. In any case, Rashi takes it to mean that everything was created on the first day, i.e., everything that was to be brought into existence was brought into existence at the beginning. In his view what happens on subsequent days is that the pre-existing entities are improved; nothing new is generated.

As we shall see, there is a sense in which what Rashi says about day one fits the rest of the account of God's initial act upon the universe. On the second day God will continue his diversification of space into distinct regions. That diversification will come to an end during the third day. From then on the divine products are all occupants of this space. Furthermore, with only two possible exceptions — the human and the Sabbath — nothing else is produced directly by God. Rather, God speaks to the spaces to generate their occupants. However, this gets ahead of our analysis of the text.

At this stage all that is clear is that there is something special about day one that separates it from the other days of God godding the world. For Rashi the difference is that on the first day, when God performs a single act of saying/seeing/separating/naming, the entire universe becomes existent. Sforno also interprets the meaning of the term "day" to be independent time. However, other classical commentators on the Hebrew text provide a time-frame.

For Nachmanides, the time of a day is the period of time of an earth day, i.e., it is what will be measurable, after God produces the sun, as a twenty-four hour period. Similarly, Ibn Ezra, as we have already mentioned, interprets a day to be the time required for the universe to undergo a complete rotation on its axis. Just how long that time period is is not specified. *Prima facie* , given that the radius of the universe is vastly greater than that of the earth and that Scripture itself says nothing about this question, there is no reason to believe that these two time periods are the same. However, this difference may only be apparent. There is no reason to assume that the velocity of these two spheres is the same. Nachmanides may accept Ibn Ezra's definition of a day and still assert that the two time periods are identical. In fact this is what Plato reports in his *Timaeus* , viz., that the length of the rotation of the motion of the Same, which rules the natural motion of the universe as a whole, is twenty-four hours.

In my judgment the most coherent reading of the biblical text itself is that all of these *prima facie* temporal terms have nothing to do with time. We have already seen that while God apparently performs multiple acts on day one, in fact there is only a single act, viz., the generation of light that makes dark actual and entails the differentiation of space into distinct elementary regions. At this stage the space itself is not yet anything. The region of earth is not as yet an earth; the region of water is not as yet seas; the region of light and dark is not as yet a sky; and there are no clear lines of demarcation between any of these territories. As such space exists, but it is not as yet something. All that has become actual is non-substantive light and dark. If what is distinctive about the first day in relation to the other days is that on the first day God generates the fundamental building blocks of the universe, then these fundamental entities are not anything at all. The fundamental universe consists of distinguishable regions of empty space, through which is found a negative dark and a separate positive light, neither of which is sharply differentiated from the other. In other words, the work of the first day, viz., the fundamental universe, has come to be, but as yet it is hardly something, and what it is is not precisely anything.

DAY 2

Genesis 1:6

ויאמר אלהים יהי רקיע בתוך המים ויהי מבדיל בין מים למים:
VA-YOMER ELOHIM YeHI RAKIYA' BeTOKH HA-MAYIM
VA-YeHIY MAVDIL BAYN MAYIM LA-MAYIM

God says, "Let there be a spread within the water to separate waters from each other."

VA-YOMER ELOHIM YeHIY, The second day begins as the first day begins, with a divine speech-act that is a command for something to be-come. On the first day the something is light. On the second day the something is called a "RAKIYA'".

"RAKIYA'" is a masculine noun that appears several times in the Hebrew Scriptures,[1] sometimes, but not always, with whatever meaning it has here. Its verbal root is resh (ר), kuf (ק), ayin (ע). The verb occurs several times in different constructions. Jeremiah uses it once in the intensive passive,[2] and Job uses it once in the causative active conjugation.[3] Job uses it to state what God does to the sky, and Jeremiah uses it to describe silver that is beaten into plates. The verb is used three times in the intensive active to express stretching and/or spreading out

---

[1] Outside of Gen 1 it occurs in Ez 1:22, 23, 25, 26; 10:1; Ps 19:2; 150:1; and Dan 12:3.
[2] Jer 10:9.
[3] Job 37:18.

one thing on something else. In Isaiah 40:19 a goldsmith spreads melted gold over an object; in Exodus 39:3 gold is beaten into thin, flat plates; and in Numbers 17:4 the priest Eleazar beats copper fire-pans into a cover for the altar.[4] The verb's most frequent use is in the simple active conjugation, where it means either "to stamp upon something with feet"[5] or "to stretch something out." Whenever it is used as Job used it, viz., with reference to God producing the universe, it means "to stretch something out." Isaiah says that "alone God NOTEH the sky, and by himself ROKA' the earth."[6] The parallelism between the two parts of the verse suggests that, as "alone" and "by himself" are parallel, so "NOTEH" and "ROKA'" are parallel. "NOTEH" means to spread or stretch something out or to expand it. In other words, God produces the universe by expanding both the sky and the earth beyond what they are at first. In fact, Isaiah associates the three verbs — BARA, NATA, and RAKA' — together when he says that "the Lord/God (HA-EL YHVH) is BORE of the sky and their expansions (NOTEY-HEM) [and] ROKA' of the earth and its progeny."[7]

The fact that the verb RAKA' parallels NOTEH in meaning "to expand," has led some scholars to translate "RAKIYA'" as "expanse."[8] Isaiah pictures the earth as a sphere (CHUG) with the sky spread out (NOTEH) around it like a curtain or tent (DOK), i.e., like a canopy.[9] Similarly, Job identifies God[10] as the one who by himself stretches out (NOTEH) the sky. On the other hand, Psalm 136:6 states that what God stretches out (ROKA') over the water is the earth. While Isaiah/Job and the Psalmist disagree about what God expands, they agree that what is expanded is an expanse. However, this translation is misleading. It suggests that a RAKIYA' is a region of space, like the domains of the

---

[4] The root appears in an alternative noun form as RIKUA' in Nu 17:3 where it has the same meaning.

[5] The verb has this meaning in Ezek 6:11; 25:6; and 2 Sam 22:43. In none of these cases is the actor God and the object the universe.

[6] Isa 44:24.

[7] Isa 42:5.

[8] Cf. Nahum M. Sarna's translation of and commentary on Gen 1:6 in *The JPS Commentary: Genesis* . Philadelphia, The Jewish Publication Society, 1989. Pg. 8.

[9] Isa 40:22.

[10] Job 9:8.

Day 2

earth and the water, which it is not. Rather, it is a new kind of stuff, like the light of the first day, that fills space.

The usual translation of "RAKIYA'" is "firmament." However, as we have seen, this English term is misleading, since the Hebrew term's referent is not itself firm and it does not make anything else firm. Rather, this RAKIYA', like its feminine noun counterpart, ReKIY'AH, is something pliable that can easily be stretched out, i.e., a ductile material. In other words, it is a kind of elastic, spread-out-able stuff, distinct from the previously listed elements, that God stretches out above the sphere earth in order to divide the encircling space of water into two distinct regions. "Stretcher" is a better translation than "firmament," because it preserves the sense that the function of this stuff, viz., stretching, defines it. However, this word has other associations in English that are not appropriate for the Hebrew. The preferred translation of the Hebrew noun is a "spread." A spread is a ductile material that is precisely what its verb expresses, viz., something of indeterminate substance[11] that someone extends over something else.

---

[11] Just what kind of "something" it is is not clear. It could be a solid (e.g., a bed spread) and/or a liquid and/or a gas and/or some other alternative. This spread will be what is called "sky," and will function to separate the dry sphere of earth from both the lower and upper spheres of water. If "earth" is the space of what is solid and "water" of what is liquid, then this spread would be something bordering on the distinction between solid and liquid. It is not unreasonable that this kind of thinking led many rabbinic commentators — e.g., R. Judah b. R. Simon and Nachmanides — to picture this spread as a kind of congealed ice. Most rabbinic commentators — e.g., Rashi, Ibn Ezra and Sforno — say that it is water solidified by the upper layer of fire heating it, i.e., it is a composite from the elements water (MAYIM) and fire (ESH). At least one commentator, viz., Gersonides, makes it a distinct kind of elementary stuff that differs radically from fire/air ($\approx$ gas), water ($\approx$ liquid), and earth ($\approx$ solid).

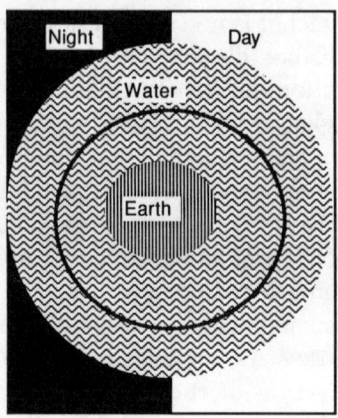

In this case the material is spread throughout the interior of the sphere of elementary water that encircles the sphere of earth, dividing two distinct areas of space into three.

Genesis 1:7

ויעש אלהים את־הרקיע
VA-YA'AS ELOHIM ET-HA-RAKIYA'
(In this way) God makes the spread

<u>VA-YA'AS ELOHIM ET-HA-RAKIYA'</u>: As God "sees" the light that he tells to be-come on the first day, so God "YA'AS" the spread that he tells to be-come here.[12] "<u>YA'AS</u>" is a shortened form of the third person, singular of the verb, 'ASAH (עשה) in the imperfect tense in the Waw Consecutive of the simple active conjugation. It has many meanings, the most important of which are "makes," "does," "works," and "acts," i.e., direct, dynamic action. It also means "produces," and as such is often associated with the act of creating (YATSAR) in general, and, more specifically, with God godding (BARA) the universe.[13] Next to "saying,"

---

[12] "Here" rather than "now" because of the atemporal character of the text's narrative.

[13] For example, Isa 41:20 says that the hand of the Lord (YHVH) made ('ASTAH) the universe and the holy one of Israel godded it (BeRA-AH). Similarly, in Isa 45:12 God says, "I made ('ASITI) earth and I godded (VARATI) man upon it."

it is the most common verb used in our text to express what God does. One reference, Isaiah 45:7, is particularly notable, because it is a regular part of Jewish worship ritual. God says in this verse that he is a "creator (YOTSER) of light and god (BORE) of dark, maker ('OSEH) of peace and god (BORE) of evil." In other words, the parallelism of the two phrases suggests that creating (YATSAR) and making ('ASAH) are the same aspect of God's godding (BARA). One verse that is especially clear about the association of these three verbs as an expression of a single divine action is Isaiah 43:7. It reads, "I godded (BeRA-TI), I created (YeTSARTI), I even made ('ASITI), everything that is called (NIKRA) by my name and my glory."[14]

ויבדל בין המים אשר מתחת לרקיע
VA-YAVDEL BAYN HA-MAYIM ASHER MeTACHAT LA-RAKIYA'
to separate the waters below the spread
ובין המים אשר מעל לרקיע
U-VAYN HA-MAYIM ASHER ME'AL LA-RAKIYA'
from the waters above the spread,

VA-YAVDEL: The third verb for God's act used here is the same verb in the same form as the third verb for God's act used on day one. As God's act of producing (= saying/seeing) the light on the first day is an act of separation, so here God's act of producing (= saying/making) the spread is an act of separation.

BAYN HA-MAYIM ASHER MeTACHAT ... U-VAYN HA-MAYIM ASHER ME'AL ...: On day one God's production of light separates light from an unproduced dark. Now God's production of a positive spread separates two regions of an unproduced water, one above and the other below the spread.

---

[14] It also indicates that naming (KARA) is part of the single divine action of creating, making and godding.

ויהי כן:

VA-YeHIY KHEN

and it becomes so.

The parallelism of verbs on day one and here continues into the next verse. As God (1) says, (2) sees (≈ makes), (3) separates, and (4) names there, here he also (1) says, (2) makes (≈ sees), (3) separates, and (4) names. However, at this point in our present verse there is a serious disruption in the pattern. On day one what God says and sees is judged good before he separates and names. Here nothing is judged to be good. Instead, <u>VA-YeHIY KHEN</u>. What is said, made and separated becomes so.

Like "TOV" and "YOM," "<u>KHEN</u>" is one of the most important technical terms in our text. It occurs six times, and, as such, it functions as a third way that God's act of producing the universe is subdivided.[15] "KHEN" is usually translated "so" or "thus," and it almost always functions logically as an expression of affirmation. Where a declarative sentence is taken to be purely descriptive, without any ontological commitment, the expression "YeHIY KHEN" functions as an existential operator. It says that what is asserted is, i.e., it declares the preceding statement to be true. In other words, both "TOV" and "KHEN" express positive value judgments about the described acts of God. "TOV" proclaims them good, while "KHEN" declares them true.

There are at least two significant differences between these two sets of value judgments in our text. First is the form of expression. Second is the content valued. Concerning the form of expression, there are two significant factors to notice. One, it is not quite correct to say that "KHEN" says that something "is." More precisely, it says that what is described is becoming something. Since the tense of the verb is imperfect, the sense of being is becoming, i.e., what is is the stable end of a dynamic process. In contrast, the expression of "good" does not use the copula in the imperfect tense. In other words, the judgment of truth

---

[15] [1] The spread separating the upper from the lower water (vs. 7) and [2] the earth's surface from the lower water (vs. 9), as well as [4] the so-called "stars" coming to be in the spread (vs. 11), as well as [3] the earth producing vegetation (vs. 11) and [5] animals (vs. 24), as well as [6] the earth's food chain (vs. 30) all are said to become so.

value is dynamic, whereas the judgment of moral value is static. While what God produces is becoming something, what it is becoming persists in being good.

Two, the judgment of moral[16] value is made by God, whereas the judgment of truth value is independent of any subject. It is God who "sees" that what he says is good. On the other hand, what God says simply becomes; the text does not say that God makes it become. In other words, the existential value judgment is independent of God and expresses something dynamic, whereas, the moral value judgment is dependent on God and expresses something permanent.

Concerning the content valued, "KHEN" and "TOV" classify in comparable but not identical ways, as the following table illustrates:

	TOV	chpt:vs	KHEN	chpt:vs
1	Light	1:04	The spread separates water	1:07
2	Seas & dry land	1:10	The spread separates seas & dry land	1:09
3	Vegetation	1:12	The earth produces vegetation	1:11
4	Lighters	1:18	The lighters enlighten the earth	1:15
5	Sea- & sky-life	1:21	The (water) earth produces life	1:24
6	Land-life	1:25	Life is food for life	1:30

Both classification systems involve most, but not all, of the same objects. Light is involved in moral, but not directly in truth, judgments; the spread is involved in truth, but not directly in moral, judgments; the fish and the birds play a more direct role in moral, than in truth, judgments. However, these are not the most important differences that the table exhibits. In general, the kinds of things that are judged to be good are entities. In contrast, the kinds of things that are judged to be true are states-of-affairs. In other words, the implicit ontology of the way our text classifies God's action is that the produced universe consists of distinct, spatially determined, dynamic states-of-affairs whose

---

[16] The term, "moral" is used here intentionally without precision. The expression "moral values" means binary value judgments in terms of good and bad, in contrast to "truth values," viz., binary value judgments in terms of true and false. As was discussed above with reference to verse 4, it is not as yet clear how the value term "good" in our text is associated with ethics.

constituent entities are defined in terms of divinely dependent, static (i.e., unchanging) moral values.

That "Va-YeHIY KHEN" occurs at this point in our narrative for the first time tells us that here, on day two, something exists for the first time. Day zero describes the state of the universe when nothing is valued or exists; day one describes the universe when something is valued — viz., the separation of day and night — but nothing exists. Now, on day two, something exists for the first time — viz., the spread that divides the water. As the next verse will assert, its name is "sky."

GENESIS 1:8

ויקרא אלהים לרקיע שמים
VA-YIKRA ELOHIM LA-RAKIYA' SHAMAYIM
God names the spread "sky,"

ויהי־ערב ויהי בקר יום שני:
VA-YeHIY-'EREV VA-YeHIY VOKER YOM SHENI
while a second day there is evening and morning.

The conclusion of the description of the second day returns to its formal parallelism with the description of day one. There God says and sees a light, which divides light from dark, that, at the conclusion of the day, he names "day" and "night" respectively. Here God says and makes a spread, which divides the water, that, at the conclusion of the day, he names "sky."

The sky is composed of the spread, as the day is composed of light, and the night of dark. Presumably the space of water is composed of

Day 2

water, and the space of earth is composed of earth.[17] These then are the five elementary materials from which the universe is composed. Three exist independent of any activity by God — water, earth, and dark. Two are produced by God for his work of creation — light and spread.

As the grammatically distinct verbs stipulated on day one describe a single divine event, so this parallel diversity of verbs describe one act by God. However, the question remains, while each act of the first two days in itself is one act, do they together constitute one or two events? In one sense, they are multiple. While the general object of God's action is the universe, that act includes a number of distinct parts, each of which has a different object.

---

[17] Later rabbinic philosophic commentaries attempt to match these elements with the elements of ancient Greek philosophy. However, there is no single match to which everyone agrees. Their views can be illustrated as follows:

Stuff	Ibn Ezra	Nachmanides	Sforno
Pre-Elemental	TOHU, BOHU	TOHU, BOHU	TOHU, BOHU, sky, earth
Elemental			
fire	air (AVIR)	dark	—
air	wind	wind	dark
water	water	water	water
earth	earth	dusk ('AFAR)	earth
celestial material	—	light	light

All of them believe that the terms "TOHU" and "BOHU" express some kind of negative stuff that is present in the universe prior to God's original act. In addition, Sforno posits all of space, viz., the sky and the earth, as primordial. All of them agree that the water named in the biblical text is the element water, and then look for other terms in the biblical account to match with the remaining classical elements. A critical term in the biblical text is "light." For all of them light is distinct from the usual four elements; it is the special divine stuff of the celestial cosmos.

Day	Created Space	Day	Created Object
1	Day, Night	4	"Stars"
2	Sky	5	Swarming-thing (of water), Flying-thing (of sky)
3	Earth	6	Living-thing (of earth), Human-thing

The first three acts differentiate distinct regions of space — day and night on day one, the sky on the second day, and (as we shall see) the earth on the third day. The next three acts differentiate distinct objects that reside within the produced space — the so-called stars in the sky on the fourth day, the living things in the water and in the sky on the fifth day, and the living things on the surface of the earth on the sixth day.[18] From this perspective, the division of the narrative into days distinguishes each divine act by the object produced.

In another sense, however, the events of each day are one. All seven days taken together constitute the single divine action stipulated in the first verse, viz., God godding the universe. In this sense, each day gives us a slightly more detailed picture of what it is that God does.

We have already seen two parts of God's product.

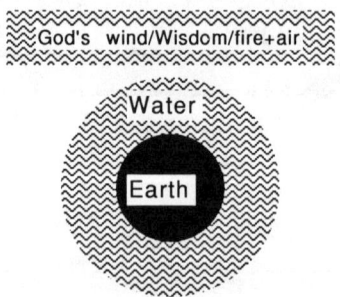

At first, i.e., at the origin of God's action, there is a dark sphere of elementary earth encompassed by a shell of elementary water that persists in a constant motion through an elementary divine wind.

The first revelation of what God does to this space is the following:

---

[18] The object created on the seventh day is the Sabbath. Just what kind of entity this is remains to be seen.

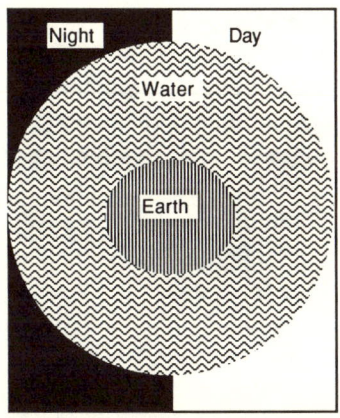

God produces a light that, in opposition to dark, pervades the entire universe. At first the passive dark is confined to the sphere of earth and the active wind is confined to the sphere of water. Here, with the production of light, the old duality of dark and wind is replaced by a new opposition of light and dark that pervades the entire universe. At first passive dark is confined to the region of earth and active divine wind is limited by the space of water. Here negative dark and positive light pervade both. At first, what is given as distinct resides in elementary space. Here, on day one, space itself resides in the divinely separated dark and light.

Next, on the second day, we see a further differentiation of space.

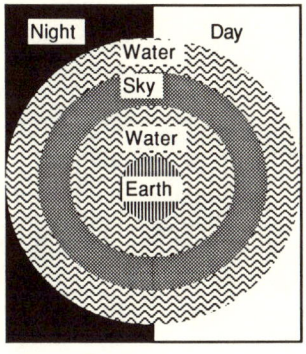

The dark and light of universe not only pervade distinct regions of earth and water; the water area itself is divided by a spreadable stuff, distinct from both earth and water. God extends this spread throughout the interior of the shell of water to form a fourth shell named "sky."

The culminating aspect of the divine act on both day one and the second day is naming. First, God names the light/dark space of day and night. Second, God names the extended space of sky. What remains for God to complete his differentiation of space into separate regions is to say and to name the seas and the land surface of the earth. This is the work of the first half of the third day.

DAY 3

Genesis 1:9

ויאמר אלהים יקוו המים מתחת השמים אל־מקום אחד

VA-YOMER ELOHIM YeKAVVU HA-MAYIM

MeTACHAT HA-SHAMAYIM EL-MAKOM ECHAD

God says, "Let the waters under the sky become collected at one place

YOMER ELOHIM: This is the third instance of God saying something. First, God tells light to be-come. Second, God tells a spread to be-come. In both of these cases God's speech act is a command for something non-existent to become existent. What God says here also is a command for something to become something. However, there is a significant difference. Here, what is commanded to become already exists. In fact, the only things that God orders into existence are the light and the spread. Everything else that God addresses already is. From this point on in our narrative, God's speech always is an order for something that is one thing to become something else. In this case, the subject is the primordial region of water. God orders the space of water to be-come collected into a single place.

<u>YeKAVVU</u> is a third person, plural imperfect tense, simple passive construction of a verb whose root consonants are kuf (ק), vav (ו), he (ה). Although the verb is used frequently in the Hebrew Scriptures in a diversity of contexts, this is the only case where it appears in this form. It means to be "collected," "gathered," or "grouped." The passive form means that the subject is to be a certain way that does not involve it actively doing anything. Furthermore, as in the previous two cases of divine commands, the imperfect tense indicates that the order is for something to be in a dynamic, rather than a static, state. The water is not commanded to <u>be</u> collected together; it is commanded to <u>become</u> this way.

<u>HA-MAYIM</u>: This is one of the few cases in our narrative that a plural number is used. However, that does not mean that God is addressing more than a single subject. The grammatical form of the word for water is dual.[1] However, the object so addressed is a single entity, viz., the space of elementary water beneath the sky.

ותראה היבשה

VA-TERA-EH HA-YAVASHAH

so that the dry-land may appear,"

When the water is collected, a "YAVASHAH" becomes perceptible. <u>YAVASHAH</u> is a feminine singular noun formed from a verb whose root is yud (י), bet (ב), shin (ש). The verb means either "to dry" something or

---

[1] The "AYIM" ending is the standard noun suffix for the dual.

for something "to be dry." Ostensibly, the noun refers to a dry object. In this case the object would be that portion of the space of earth that no longer is encompassed by the water, that, instead, is directly encompassed by the spread of the sky. In other words, "YAVASHAH" is earth that no longer is wet, i.e., it is what becomes dry-land.

There are two possible ways that this dry-land can be formed. One possibility is that the space of the sky and/or the earth expand. Another possibility is that the territory of the water contracts. The first alternative is suggested in the names of rabbis Acha, Isaac, Nathan, and Berekiah in the *Genesis Rabbah* commentary on this verse. However, the latter alternative is more likely the intent of the narrative, since the object addressed by the divine speech act is the water, not the earth or the sky. Presumably, the contraction of the water results in the upper surface of the sphere of earth emerging beyond the sphere of the water into the sky. In either case, the space of the universe at this stage of the narrative would have something like the following structure:

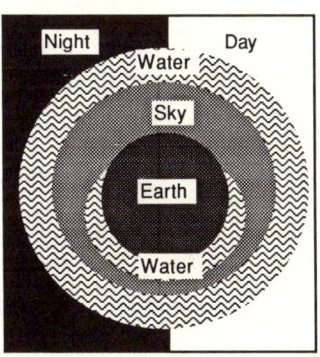

:וַיְהִי־כֵן

VA-YeHIY-KHEN
and it becomes so.

The division of the water into an upper and a lower region by the spread was said to become so. Now the separation of the dry from the wet portion of the earth is said to become so. This second truth judgment precedes any moral judgment, which indicates that it was not quite accurate to call the dry-land an "object." God only makes two objects — the light of day and the spread of the sky. In contrast, "dry-land" is not something made. Rather, the term expresses a state-of-affairs about the pre-existing earth, viz., that there is a portion of its space that becomes dry and is not permeated by water. The question is, what object is it becoming? The answer is given in the next verse.

Genesis 1: 10

ויקרא אלהים ליבשה ארץ ולמקוה המים קרא ימים

VA-YIKRA ELOHIM LA-YAVASHAH ARETZ UL-MIKVEH HA-MAYIM KARA YAMIM

God names the dry-land "earth" and names the collection of waters "seas,"

God names something for the third time. First, he names the light and dark "day" and "night" respectively. Second, he names the spread that divides the waters "sky." Now he names the dry and wet areas beneath the sky "earth" and "seas" respectively. The term for earth, ARETZ, at this stage of the narrative means the land mass of the planet earth. It is the same as the term that has been used until now for both the element earth and the primordial space of that element. That the same word is used indicates the relationship between the space, the element and the object. In reality they constitute a single thing, viz., space that disposes a primordial element that at first is nothing that, through its disposition, is becoming an object. The object is what is named. Names express positive ideals towards which the original negative entities are ordered by God's speech act to come to be. Similarly, the term, <u>YAMIM</u> names an object, viz., the seas, towards which the space of the elementary water beneath of the sky disposes the primordial elementary water to come to be.

וירא אלהים כי־טוב:

VA-YAR ELOHIM KI-TOV
while God perceives that it is excellent.

God perceives, and thus, judges, the named objects — earth and seas — to be excellent. This perception completes God's unique action upon the space of the universe. It is an act of judgment that, as such, means that these objects are ideals, rather than actualities, that function as limit-ends for the now separate, primordial spaces, filled with their original stuff, to strive to become. Consequently, the final picture of the space of the universe, prior to that space generating its occupants, is not a description of what the universe literally looks like. Rather, it is a geometric model of the divinely fixed end of the space of this universe. How this model is intended to function readily can be illustrated by the way that calculus is used in geometry and physics.

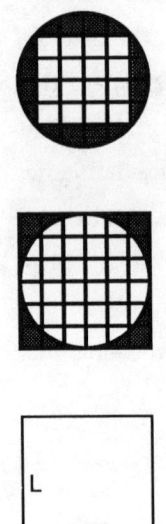

The area of a circle is determined to be p multiplied by the radius squared (A = pr²). A circle is defined as "the limit of areas of inscribed (or circumscribed) regular polygons as the number of sides increase without bound."[2] First, inscribe a circle with a set of rectangles, the area of each of which is easily measurable as length (L) times width (W), and add up the sum of these areas. Second, circumscribe the circle with a set of rectangles and add up the sum of their areas. The first set will be smaller and the second set larger than the actual area of the circle. (The area in error is darkened.) As the width of the rectangles in each set decreases, the number of individual rectangles in the two sums will increase, and the closer each set will come to the actual area of the circle. (In other words, the darkened area in error will decrease.)

In this instance, the ideal of measurement is zero. Zero is ideal,

---

[2] Thomas, George B. Jr. and Finney, Ross L. *Calculus and Analytic Geometry*. Reading, MA, Addison-Wesley Publishing Co., 1981. Pg. 188.

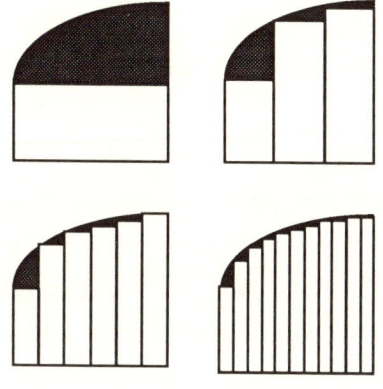

because the closer the measurement of the width of each rectangle comes to zero, the closer the sum of areas is to the area of the circle. Furthermore, zero is not actual, because the area of any rectangle of zero width is zero,[3] and the sum of zero areas is zero.[4] Carrying out this procedure — viz., determining a set of sums of rectangles that either inscribe or circumscribe a circle, where the width of each rectangle continuously approximates, but does not in fact reach, zero — results in the general formula, $A = pr^2$ for determining the actual area of any circle. The same procedure is involved in determining the volume of a sphere.[5] Here the resulting general formula is $(4/3)pr^3$. In effect, something actual, viz., the volume of a sphere, is dependent on something ideal, viz., the calculation of a dynamic process of reducing something towards an in-principle, unrealizable limit.

Newton's three laws of motion are examples of the use of this kind of mathematics in thinking about the dynamics of physical bodies. The first law states that if the vector sum of forces on a body is zero, then the acceleration of the body also is zero. The second law expresses a ratio between the force and the acceleration when the vector sum of the forces is not zero. The third law expresses the ratio between pairs of forces that

---

[3] The area (A) of a rectangle is its length (L) times its width (W), i.e. $A = L \times W$. Let L equal any number, n, greater than zero. $A = n \times 0 = 0$.
[4] $0 + 0 + ... + 0 = 0$.
[5] Volume is the counterpart in three dimensional space to area in two dimensional space; a sphere is the three dimensional counterpart of a two dimensional circle.

interacting bodies exert on each other. For our purposes, the second law is most significant, because it expresses the ratio between force (F) and acceleration (a) that defines mass (m), viz., $m = F/a$. In other words, the "stuff" of physical objects in Newtonian physics, viz., their mass, is quite different from the "stuff" of Aristotelian physics, viz., matter. Aristotelian matter is not anything at all, since form is what makes any object be something. Nonetheless, it still is a thing, viz., a kind of substance. In contrast, Newtonian mass is not a thing. Rather, what it is is defined mathematically as a ratio between two different kinds of vectors, viz., a body's acceleration and a sum of its forces. What is critical is that the elements in defining mass are vectors, viz., directions with magnitude, neither of which can be called "things."

In sum, the space of the physical universe that God produces on the first three days of the Genesis narrative of creation is not any-thing at all. Rather, it is dynamic space, separated into distinct regions with distinct powers of their own. These dynamic regions are night, day, water above the sky, sky, and earth and water below the sky. These regions are formed from God producing two kinds of stuff — light and spread — to interact with three primordial kinds of stuff — dark, water and earth.

Except for the light and the spread, God's unique action upon the universe involves making separations. The separations enable God to name things, viz., night and day, sky, earth and seas. These divine names refer to ideal objects that function as limit-ends towards which space itself moves. What is is in constant motion to become what it ought to be. Classical rabbinic commentators interpreted the implicit ontology of Genesis in terms of Aristotelian science. The named limits were taken to express forms that inhere in the stuff of the universe. This stuff was interpreted in terms of Aristotelian hyle and four or five fundamental elements. However, the fit is far from perfect. The most critical point of disparity between the implicit ontology of the Genesis narrative and Aristotelian physics turns on the category of substance. Aristotelianism saw the universe primarily in static terms. Nouns as subjects and adjectives as attributes that modify the subjects dominate the linguistic model that yields a fundamentally static picture of the universe. In contrast, verbs as actions dominate our narrative, and yield a fundamentally dynamic model. Space is prior to what occupies space, and things function primarily as fixed, ideal ends for what in actuality is movement in a direction. While there is a certain amount of coherence between Aristotelian forms and the integral limits in Newton's use of calculus, there is a radical incoherence between the relative roles of Aristotelian matter and Newtonian mass in characterizing the fundamental stuff of the physical universe. Matter is a kind of something that is nothing. Mass cannot be thought of in these terms. It expresses that what is has to be understood, not as things subject to change but, as a ratio of directed movements. Biblical space, like Newtonian mass, is a given, whose intelligibility (expressed through separations) is a direction commanded by God.

The Genesis account of creation can be divided into two main parts: The differentiation of space and the generation of its occupants. The first part is complete. Until now our text revealed the division of dynamic space, produced directly through divine speech. From now on the narrative uncovers the classification of the living occupants of space, generated directly by space itself in response to divine command. In general, what God does to space is make distinctions — day and night, upper and lower water, and dry-land and the seas. More separations remain to be drawn. As God separates night and day above the sky, and dry-land and seas below the sky, so the second part of the narrative distinguishes the human from other forms of life below the sky, and the time of the Sabbath from the time of other days. These are the only separations explicitly mentioned in our text. However, more will be drawn after creation. Israel will be distinguished from the rest of humanity, Levites from Israelites, and priests from Levites. Similarly, the land of Israel will be distinguished from the rest of the earth, Jerusalem from Israel, the temple mount from Jerusalem, and the space of the Holy of Holies from the rest of the temple. All of these distinctions will be perceived by the deity of the Hebrew Scriptures to have positive value.

Genesis 1:11

ויאמר אלהים תדשא הארץ דשא

VA-YOMER ELOHIM TADSHE HA-ARETZ DESHE

God says, "Let the earth sprout a sprout

This is the fourth instance of God performing a speech-act that functions as an imperative. However, this case differs from the others in two significant respects. First, the actions in the previous three cases were intended to differentiate regions of space, viz., producing light to distinguish day from night, producing the spread of the sky to distinguish the upper and lower waters, and collecting water to distinguish the land from the seas. In this case God produces something that occupies space, viz., vegetation.

Day 3

Second, God is the only actor in the previous three cases. In this instance something else acts. The commands in the first two cases are not directed to any subject. God exhorts light to become and a spread to become, but there is nothing already there commanded to become either.[6] In the third case there is a subject, viz., the water. However, the water is not commanded to do anything. Rather it is ordered to let something happen to it, viz., become collected. The present case is radically different. Here something already existent, viz., the earth, is commanded to do something, viz., produce vegetation.

I take the subject of God's command, <u>HA-ARETZ</u>, to refer to the earth, viz., the primordial spatial region filled with elementary earth, and not the land, viz., that part of the earth that is distinguishable from the seas. The reason for this choice is that vegetation exists in the seas as well as on the land mass of the earth.

Most classical rabbinic commentators[7] on the Hebrew Scriptures say that it is the angels, not the earth, who are commanded to produce vegetation. Clearly this is not what our text says. The source of their misreading may be the following: All of them were to some extent committed to an Aristotelian world view in which it is unintelligible to say that space can act. The givens are that God commands something other than himself to produce vegetation, the subject addressed by God's imperative must be a substance, spatial regions are not substances, and the only things that have been produced so far are spaces. From this data they conclude that God must be addressing substances that are not

---

[6] In this restricted sense it can be said about our narrative that God creates the world out of nothing.

[7] One exception to the following generalization is Nachmanides, who claims that this verse means that the earth is predisposed with a potentiality or power (KOACH) to generate vegetation.

mentioned in our narrative because they are eternal entities, viz., angels. The same issue arises in connection with verses 20 through 25 where *prima facie* the earth and the water are commanded to generate life forms. However, clearly, it is to the earth that God addresses his command. Hence, there is every reason to believe that the author(s) of our narrative were not Aristotelians, since the implied ontology and physics underlying this story admits the possibility that space can act.

The command given to the earth is TADSHE ... DESHE. The verb and the noun have the same root, viz., daled (ד), shin (ש), aleph (א). The noun, <u>DESHE</u> occurs here in the singular. It can mean "grass," "herbage," "vegetation," "ground cover," and/or "a sprout." Whichever English term is most appropriate depends on two factors. First, the noun refers to something whose characteristic operation is what the verb expresses. Second, the term has close associations with the words "'ESEV" and "'ETS."

The verb, <u>TADSHE</u> is a third person, feminine, singular form of the imperfect tense of the causative, simple active construction. This is its sole appearance in the Hebrew Scriptures in this form, and it occurs only one other time in a different form. In Joel 2:22 the verb is a third person, plural form in the perfect tense of the simple active construction. The Joel passage says that the pastures of the wilderness "DASH-U" [just as] a tree bears (NASA) its fruit. The causative form means, to cause something to do whatever DASH-A is. If the noun is "vegetation", then the verb is "to cause to vegetate." Similarly, if the noun is "a sprout," then the verb is "to cause to sprout." The latter expression makes more sense than the former in our text. To vegetate is passive, "to sprout" is active, and what God exhorts the earth to produce here is something active. In other words, the earth is commanded to make a sprout sprout.

עֵשֶׂב מַזְרִיעַ זֶרַע עֵץ פְּרִי עֹשֶׂה פְּרִי לְמִינוֹ אֲשֶׁר זַרְעוֹ־בוֹ עַל־הָאָרֶץ
'ESEV MAZRIYA' ZERA' 'ETZ PeRI 'OSEH PeRI
Le-MINO ASHER ZAR'O-BO 'AL-HA-ARETZ
of plant that seeds seed, (and) of fruit-tree that makes fruit of its own kind,
that contains its seed within itself through the earth,"

Through the power of the earth, the sprout is to sprout two kinds of things. The first is an 'ESEV, and the second is an 'ETZ PeRI. In other words, there are two kinds of things that a sprout sprouts. One is an 'ESEV and the other is an 'ETZ PeRI. Every commentator on this text recognizes that the terms "DESHE," "'ESEV," and "'ETZ PeRI" are interrelated, and that this verse deals with the origin of all kinds of vegetation. However, at a more specific level, there is little agreement about what these terms mean. For example, Rashi says that DESHE is ground cover, and 'ESEV is its roots; Sforno says that DESHE and 'ESEV are two different terms for grass; and Nachmanides says that DESHE and 'ESEV mean plants in general, DESHE being a collective term for what as individual species are called 'ESEV. Furthermore, although Rashi says that 'ETZ PeRi refers to trees that taste like fruit (as opposed to trees that have fruit), most other commentators agree that 'ETZ PeRI refers to fruit bearing trees. However, they never specify if the phrase refers exclusively to trees that bear fruit or to all kinds of fruit-bearing plants.[8]

---

[8] For example, is a tomato plant an instance of an 'ETZ PeRI?

An 'ESEV is either grass, an herb, or a weed. An 'ETZ is a tree or wood. Both are plants, each of which "seeds⁹ seed" (MAZRIYA' ZERA'), i.e., causes its seed to perform the characteristic act of seed, viz., to sprout forth from the earth and grow into new members of its species. An 'ETZ PeRI is a plant that bears fruit. The text tells us that it makes its own kind of fruit. "Its own kind" (Le-MINO) means that apple trees will only make apples, peach trees peaches, date trees dates, ..., but apple trees do not make peaches or dates ..., and peach trees do not make apples or dates ..., etc. What distinguishes an 'ETZ PeRI from an 'ESEV is the following: The ovary that encompasses the seed ("ASHER ZAR'O-BO") of an 'ETZ PeRI is fruit, whereas (by implication) in an 'ESEV it is not. "Fruit" (PeRI) is something edible. Hence, the earth is commanded to empower a sprout to sprout two kinds of plants: those whose ovaries are not fruit and those whose ovaries are fruit. The former, 'ESEV, simply refers to plants. The latter, 'ETZ PeRI, refers to fruit-trees, where "trees" should be understood to be fruit bearing plants.

Note that all plants have ovaries that encompass their seed, and every plant reproduces only members of its own species. Hence, the expressions, "its own kind" (Le-MINO) and "that contains its seed within itself" (ASHER ZAR'O-BO) refer to both kinds of plants, and not just to a fruit plant. Similarly, the concluding phrase, "'AL-HA-ARETZ" refers to both kinds of plant. What does the sprouting is a sprout, but it is the earth that empowers a sprout to perform its characteristic function. This relationship between a sprout and the earth is expressed by the phrase, "'AL-HA-ARETZ." Almost always the preposition, 'AL, in this

---

⁹ "MAZRIYA'" is a masculine, singular active participle of the causative, active participle of a verb whose root is zayin (ז), resh (ר), kuf (ק). The noun, ZERA' has the same root.

Day 3   67

verse is translated as "upon," meaning either that the fruit tree is to be set on the land and/or its seed is to be cast upon the land, or, in more general terms, that the product of a sprout sprouting, viz., vegetation, is commanded to be upon the land. Of these three alternatives, the third is the best. However, none of these interpretations adequately expresses what the text says. On these interpretations "HA-ARETZ" refers solely to the dry-land, which excludes the seas. Since no command is given to the seas to sprout sprouts within the water, either the author(s) did not know that the seas also contain vegetation, or "'AL-HA-ARETZ" has a different meaning. The latter alternative is more likely. If the preposition means "by means of" or "through (the agency of)" the earth, then this verse asserts what we would infer to be the case anyway, viz., that our text identifies the spatial element earth as the source of the power of vegetation to reproduce, in the seas as well as on the land.

ויהי־כן:

VA-YeHIY-KHEN

and it becomes so.

While the terms "DESHE," "'ESEV" and "ETZ PeRI" refer to a multiplicity of plants — DESHE to sprouts, 'ESEV to plants, and 'ETZ PeRI' to fruit-plants — this is not what the words mean, mainly because the noted referents are pluralities while each term is singular. "DESHE" is a sprout, not sprouts; 'ESEV is a plant, not plants; 'ETZ PeRI is a fruit-tree, not fruit trees. Hence, what comes to be on day three are not all the plants and vegetation of the land and the seas. Rather, the earth is commanded to sprout a single sprout, that can become a plant, that can seed a seed, encompassed by something that is and/or is not fruit.[10] Furthermore, the state of affairs that comes to be is not that plants produce plants. Rather, it is the earth that is the source of the ability of plants to reproduce. What comes to be here is not an object; what comes to be is a truth judgment, viz., that vegetation derives its ability to reproduce from elementary earth-space.

Genesis 1:12

ותוצא הארץ דשא עשב מזריע זרע למינהו

VA-TOTZE HA-ARETZ DESHE 'ESEV MAZRIYA' ZERA' Le-MINO

The earth produces a sprout of a plant that seeds seed of its own kind,

God tells the earth to sprout a sprout of plant that seeds seed, and of fruit-tree that makes fruit. Then the earth "TOTZE" a plant that seeds seed. There are three questions to raise about this first half of the verse. First, what happened to the fruit-tree? Second, what kind of act does "TOTZE" express? Third, what does "then" mean?

The preceding verse said that two kinds of plants will grow out of the first sprout, one kind whose seed is encased in fruit and another kind whose seed is not encased in fruit. Here the term "'ESEV" functions at a more general level for both kinds of plants. It does not mean that the earth sprouts only the non-fruit bearing, seeded plant.

---

[10] That the earth produces a single prototype that produces two subtypes occurs again in the second half of Gen 1:27 where God gods a single thing, viz., the human, who is male and/or female. Both R.F. Pfeiffer (in *Introduction to the Old Testament* . New York, 1941) and U. Cassuto (in *A Commentary on the Book of Genesis*. Jerusalem, 1961) emphasized the structural parallelism between the plant and the human in the Genesis account of creation.

TOTZE is a third person, singular of the imperfect tense in the causative active construction of a verb whose root is yud (י), tsadik (צ), aleph (א). The verb appears in this form only two more times in the Hebrew Scriptures — in Genesis 1:24 and in Ruth 2:18. In Genesis 1:24 the earth once again is the actor. In Genesis 1:12 the act results in a sprout; in Genesis 1:24 the result is a living thing. Ruth 2:18 gives us more insight into just what kind of act this is. After gleaning a certain amount of barley from a field, Ruth lifts it up, brings it to the city, shows it to her mother-in-law, and then she "TOTZE" and gives what she does not need for her personal use to her mother-in-law. In Ruth's case the product is a left-over. The verb means that she separates out for herself what she is going to use in order to do something else to (viz., give away) the remainder. Hence, TOTZE involves an active agent doing one thing in preparation for doing something else.

The simple active construction of the verb has a great many different meanings, including to "go out" and/or "come out" and/or "emerge" and/or "appear" and/or "arise" and/or "leave" and/or "depart". The causative active form does not mean to do any of these things; rather, it means to cause or dispose these acts to occur. In the Ruth case, the verb means that Ruth acts with intent in such a way that she has the ability to give something to her mother-in-law, viz., to make something that is intended to "leave" or "depart" from her. In other words, she "produces" the remainder to be able to give it away. Similarly, in the two cases in Genesis the earth acts in a certain way that disposes itself to cause something that it possesses to go out, come out, emerge, appear, arise, leave and/or depart from it. In verse 12, the "something" is vegetation. Later it will be a higher order of life form. In both cases what the earth produces is a prototype of a species. In neither case does it actually produce any members of the species.

Hence, in response to God's command, the earth produces a single prototype of all kinds of plants, through which it subsequently can give away an endless number of individual plants. Once again, this verse does not say that the earth brings forth plants. Rather, it says that the earth produces a single thing within itself that empowers it to cause plants to sprout forth. Consequently, this sprout is not a sprout, and this plant is not a plant. Rather, it is a model for the earth to generate all sprouts and all plants.

It follows from the above analysis that this "VA," like all the others we have seen so far, does not mean "afterwards." The earth producing a disposition within itself to generate vegetation is a consequence of God telling the earth to so dispose itself. In this sense "VA" means "then." However, it is not the case that first God orders the earth and then the earth obeys God's command. As God ordering a spread to come to be is simultaneous with God making the spread, so God ordering the earth to begin to sprout a sprout is simultaneous with the earth producing a sprout.

וירא אלהים כי־טוב:

VA-YAR ELOHIM KI-TOV

while God perceives that it is excellent.

Similarly, as God ordering light to become is simultaneous with God perceiving that it is excellent, and so God ordering the earth to produce a plant is simultaneous with God perceiving it to be excellent. This is the third instance of God perceiving an ideal object. The first was light. The second was dry-land and seas. The third is vegetation. All three objects are "ideal" in the sense just explained for the vegetation. They are prototypes within space that empower the space continuously to act in a certain way. Only in the case of vegetation are we told what that "way" is, viz., to enable its space to generate innumerable individual plants.

Genesis 1:13

ויהי־ערב ויהי בקר יום שלישי:

VA-YeHIY-'EREZ VA-YeHIY VOKER YOM SHeLISHI

A third day there is evening and morning.

At first there is a sphere of dark, passive earth encompassed by a sphere of active water. On day one, God produces light, which, together with the pre-produced dark, divides the space of the universe into regions of day and night. On the second day, God produces a spread named sky that divides the pre-produced water into two distinct regions. On the third day, God orders the lower region of water to be collected in such a way that a part of the earth sphere emerges from the sphere of water to form a separation within the composite globe of elementary earth and water between regions named land and seas.

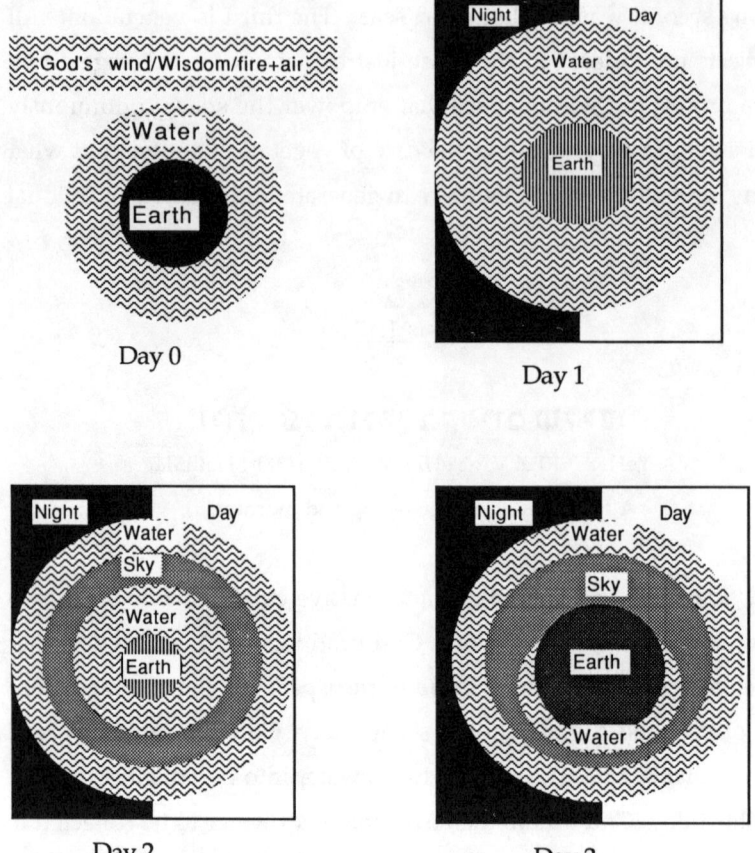

Day 0

Day 1

Day 2

Day 3

This divine act completes the differentiation of space. The universe is divided into regions of earth, seas, sky and waters above the sky that together are divided into regions of day and night. Together the three days form a single picture of space. As yet there is nothing in space, and there is no time. The third day also begins the description of the prototypes of the occupants of space. The earth is ordered to produce a sprout from which all vegetation will come to be. This enfolding model of the universe will continue with prototypes for the sky, as well as life on the land and in the seas. This work will continue through the sixth day.

DAY 4

Genesis 1:14

ויאמר אלהים יהי מארת
VA-YOMER ELOHIM YeHIY MeOROT
God says, "Let there be lighters

VA-YOMER ... YeHIY: This is the third instance of God telling something to be-come. The first is the light on day one. The second is the spread on the second day. What God says into existence here are MeOROT. These three entities — light, spread and MeOROT — are the only three entities that God produces directly through his speech-act. Light's opposite, dark, exists independent of God's action, as do the spaces of the water and the earth that the spread separates into earth, seas, sky, and upper-water. Everything else[1] is produced directly by the spaces themselves.

MeOROT is a plural form of the masculine noun MAOR. It has the same root — aleph (א), vav (ו), resh (ר) — as the term, OR, for the light produced on day one. The plural ending, "OT" usually indicates a feminine noun. The noun's sole appearance in the feminine plural is in our narrative. In its only other appearance in the Hebrew Scriptures, the noun's plural form is masculine.[2] In this related text, Ezekiel, speaking of Israel's impending destruction, reports God to say that he will cover over

---

[1] With the possible exception of the human.
[2] In Ez 32:8.

the sky (SHAMAYIM) by blackening its celestial-objects (KOKHAVEYHEM), covering the sun (SHEMESH) with a cloud and preventing the moon (YAREACH) from giving light.[3] God repeats this threat in the next verse by saying that he will blacken all the MeOREI[4] of light in the sky, and he will set dark (CHOSHEKH) upon the land (ERETZ).[5]

As the feminine form of the plural of the noun MAOR occurs only in our narrative, so the masculine form of the plural occurs only in the Ezekiel passage cited. The context in both cases suggests that the plural of MAOR has the same reference. What it is is suggested by Ezekiel's concrete reference to the moon. He tells us that this MAOR usually "YAIR" its light.[6] "YAIR" is a third person, masculine, singular in the imperfect tense of the causative, active construction of our verbal root, which means, to make light, i.e., to enlighten. Hence, the plural of MAOR refers to a set of objects, like the sun and the moon, that make the light of the sky enlighten space, such as the earth, without which that space is pervaded by dark. Light and dark are a kind of stuff. In this respect they are like water, earth and the spread. However, whereas the latter three elements are restricted to only certain regions of space, the light and the dark pervade the entire universe.

ברקיע השמים
BeRAKIYA' HA-SHAMAYIM
in the spread of the sky

We are told on day one that light and dark are separate, but we were not told how they are separate. So far we have exhibited that separation as a division of all space. However, now it is clear that this way of picturing the division is in an important respect misleading. It is not the case that some space is dark and other space is light, as some space is filled with elementary water and other space with elementary earth. Rather, dark and light fill all space in the sense that all space can be, independent of the other elements that fill it, light or dark. What

---

[3] Ez 32:7.

[4] The masculine plural construct form of the noun MAOR.

[5] Ez 32:8.

[6] Ez 32:7.

makes space in actuality one or the other is the function of the MeOROT. When present these objects cause space to be light; when absent or covered that same space is dark. Hence, MeOROT are "lighters," i.e., objects that cause space to be enlightened.

It is now clear that the sense in which light and dark are separate on the first three days of creation is not that some space is in actuality light while other space is in actuality dark. Rather, light and dark are distinct potentials within all of space. Hence, it is also clear how the picture that Genesis draws of the universe is to be interpreted. It is not a historical picture, i.e., it is not the case that the universe looked a certain way on day one, then it looked a different way on the second day, etc. Rather, our picture is not a picture at all. It is a model for understanding the original nature of our present universe. Each day adds another layer of detail to our model. But what the model models is, with respect to time, always there.

להבדיל בין היום ובין הלילה
Le-HAVDIL BAYN HA-YOM U-VAYN HA-LAYLAH
to separate the day from the night,

Lighters come to be in the sky for a purpose. That purpose is to separate day and night. Hence, the prior distinction between day and night is not yet actual. Rather, it is a potential within all of space to be subject to day and night. The purpose of the lighters is to activate both potentialities in the space of the universe.

והיו לאתת ולמועדים ולימים ושנים:
Ve-HAYU Le-OTOT UL-MO'ADIM UL-YAMIM Ve-SHANIM
to have signs, seasons, days and years.

Day and night also are not ends in themselves. They too have a purpose, viz. to become OTOT, MO'ADIM, YAMIM and SHANIM. OTOT is the plural of a noun whose singular form is "OT." An OT is a sign, a mark, a signal, and/or a banner. In linguistics it is a token; in semantics it is what a word indicates. It can also be an emblem. What God places on the head of Cain to identify him to the rest of the world as

Cain is an OT.[7] Its function is to tell the world that this is Cain and he is to be treated differently from everyone else, viz., he is not to be killed and he is not allowed to establish a permanent residence. Similarly, God tells all of Israel to make flags that have "marks" that identify each individual's family/tribe.[8] These marks are called "OTOT." In general, OTOT mark something off for special notice, that otherwise might pass unnoticed, for special treatment.

MO'ADIM are set times or seasons for special meetings. During the period of the first two Jewish political states, the term referred to the times designated under Toraitic law for the nation to meet together at the Temple to offer special sacrifices. Throughout the Hebrew Scriptures the word functions as a general term for all of the festivals, most notably, Sukkot, Pesach and Shavuot.

The meaning of the last two words in this phrase seems easiest to interpret. YAMIM are days, and SHANIM are years. Presumably, the planet earth and/or the sky rotates in a regular way, so that each complete cycle of their relative movement constitutes a way to reckon a temporal unit called a "day," while a fixed number of such days counts to reckon a larger unit called a "year." On this interpretation, "seasons" are the seasons of the year, which are the first-level subdivision of the year, viz., spring, summer, fall, and winter.

Note that these are ways of reckoning time, and as such, these days, contrary to the day and night of the rest of our narrative, have no ontological status. Our previous "day" and "night" are names of stuff, viz., light and dark respectively, that characterize space, independent of any temporal reference. The days referred to here in this verse do not exist. Rather, they are part of a language for calculating the number of cycles of motion in space.

While this interpretation of days and years is most obvious, it is not most likely to be the correct interpretation. First, on this interpretation the text should list days first, since both years and seasons depend on the unit of days. Second, it makes no sense out of the term "signs."

Undoubtedly this textual problem was one reason why the early rabbinic commentators sought alternate interpretations. *Genesis Rabbah* reports that the sages used the common sense meaning of

---

[7] Gen 4:15.
[8] Nu. 2:2.

"seasons" as the pilgrim festivals of Sukkot, Pesach, and Shavuot to interpret the other temporal designations as well. They include Sabbath with the seasons, take "years" to refer to Rosh Ha-Shanah, and "days" to mean "new moons." What is most interesting about their interpretation is that the lighters in the sky are produced ultimately for ritual purposes. However, even this interpretation fails to make sense out of the term for signs.

On Rashi's interpretation "signs" are evil-omens. Presumably what he had in mind is the following: The movement of the lighters is sufficiently regular for human beings to be able to calculate periods of time. These calculations ultimately serve ritual purposes, viz., they enable people to determine when to fulfill special obligations. "Special" means obligations that do not apply all of the time. Normally people are to work, but one day out of seven, the Sabbath, they are to rest. Normally people may eat leavened bread, but seven/eight days out of the year, viz., during Pesach, they may only eat unleavened bread, etc. However, even these "special" times are normal in the sense that they recur at regular intervals. In addition, there are even less normal, more special times, viz., unique banner events whose singularity marks them off for special recognition, as a distinctive flag standing above a group of people can mark them off for unique identity. Within the realm of nature such events could be eclipses of the sun and the moon, or conjunctions of planets and constellations. Such repeating, but much less regular, celestial events could have special significance. As such they are called "OTOT," viz., signs that may portend momentous happenings that may be, as Rashi seemed to think, evil, but might also be good, e.g., the coming of the age of the Messiah.

These special functions at these times separate these time periods from other periods of time. We have already noted that the main thing God does in producing the universe is make distinctions. The lighters enable human beings to continue the divine activity of making separation within the universe that God produces.

In sum, at this stage of revelation our model of the original universe has been modified in three significant ways. First, the objects that occupy space serve purposes beyond themselves. They are not static. Rather, they have continuous motion, and that motion is to be conceived as a vector that has direction. The lighters' coming to be points to the end of enabling humans to distinguish some periods of time from others.⁹ Second, objects are set in the space of the spread. Their presence makes their individual domain of space light, while the regions that do not fall under the influence of any lighter remain dark. Third, the full extent of the universe consists of a series of enclosed spheres with earth at the center, surrounded by water and spread, surrounded by the spread of the sky, surrounded by the upper water. In itself space is dark. It becomes light only when it is subject to the influence of the sky's lighters. How these lighters divide space into day and night becomes clearer in the next four verses.

<u>Genesis 1:15</u>

והיו למאורת ברקיע השמים להאיר על־הארץ
Ve-HAYU LIMeOROT Be-RAKIYA' HA-SHAMAYIM Le-HA-IR 'AL-HA-ARETZ
The lighters within the spread of the sky have (power) to enlighten the earth,"

The text does not say that the lighters enlighten the surface of the earth. Rather, it says "<u>HAYU LI</u>", viz., that they have the ability or power or potentiality to do so. In general, all of the characteristics that our narrative attributes to spaces and spatial objects are dispositions. This sense is built into this use of the verb "to be" as it functions in our narrative. The universe described is not the actual universe; rather, it is a model for understanding what continuously occurs in our universe. This is another reason why it is a mistake to understand the actions described on each day as temporal events.

The expression <u>Le-HA-IR 'AL-Ha-ARETZ</u> specifies the region of space subject to the enlightening power of the lighters. It is the land, viz., the surface of the globe of the earth that faces the spread of the sky, that becomes light and dark. Light and dark, and hence day and night, are restricted to this domain. It does not apply to the space of the universe in general. Hence, the upper waters should be understood to be neither dark nor light, i.e., they are not permeated by either element. Rather, the stuff of this region of space is elementary water.

---

⁹ The purpose of the first generated occupants of space, the vegetation, remains to be seen.

Day 4   81

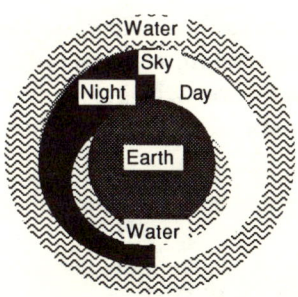

What is problematic in our text is whether or not the domain of the lighters' influence also extends to the surface of the lower waters that face the sky. The same question can be asked about the earth producing vegetation, viz., does it only produce vegetation at its surface facing the sky or does it also produce it at its surface facing the seas. A most literal reading of our text would suggest the narrower interpretation, viz., it is only the dry-land that becomes enlightened and grows plants. However, it is hard to picture this interpretation, given that the entire globe of earth and water is surrounded by sky, and that the relative position of this central globe to its surrounding ring of sky is subject to a regular cycle of change. Furthermore, it seems unlikely that the author(s) of our narrative did not know that there are plants in the seas and/or that one still experiences day and night while at sea. Hence, the broader interpretation is more likely to be the intended picture, viz., vegetation grows at every surface of the earth and the lighters within the sky enlighten the surface of the entire central globe of the universe, both the dry-land and the seas.

Furthermore, the term <u>HA-ARETZ</u> has a broader meaning here than it has had previously in our narrative. At first it referred to one of the elementary kinds of stuff that fill unoccupied-by-objects space. On the third day it becomes the name for the surface of that subdivision of the universe's central globe that is filled with earth. Now, on the fourth day, it is used to refer to the surface of the entire central globe, composed of both elementary earth and water.

ויהי־כן:
VA-YeHIY-KHEN
and it becomes so.

This is the fourth instance of something coming to be so. On the second day, the spread separates the waters into two regions. On the third day, two additional dynamic states-of-affairs come to be. First, the spread is extended to separate the seas from the dry land at the surface of the universe's central globe of water and earth. Second, the earth-space is empowered to produce vegetation at its surface. Now, on the fourth day, the lighters situated in the spread-space are empowered to produce light at that same surface where vegetation will grow. The purpose of this celestial empowerment is explained in the next three verses.

Genesis 1:16

ויעש אלהים את־שני המארת הגדלים
VA-YA'AS ELOHIM ET-SHeNAI HA-MeOROT HA-GeDOLIM
God makes two large lighters,

This verse specifies the kind of lighters that God's speech-act in verse 14 produces. It does not assert a distinct act. It is not the case that first God orders (YOMER) lighters and then he makes (YA'AS) them into different kinds. Rather, the ordering and the making express the same action.

את־המאור הגדל לממשלת היום ואת־המאור הקטן לממשלת הלילה
ET-HA-MA-OR HA-GADOL Le-MAMSHELET HA-YOM
Ve-ET-HA-MA-OR HA-KATAN Le-MAMSHELET HA-LAYLAH
(viz.,) the large lighter for governing the day, and the small lighter for governing the night,

Two lighters in particular are singled out for mention. They are distinguished by their size. By general consensus, the so-called "large" one is the sun, and the so-called "small" one is the moon. Why they are singled out, however, has nothing to do with their size.[10] Rather, they have a distinct purpose, viz., to establish a "MAMSHELET" over day and night.

The preposition Le in this case expresses purpose. God makes the two lighters "for the sake of," i.e., for the purpose of, something. That something is a state-of-affairs, viz., "MAMSHELET" day and night. MAMSHELET is the construct form of the noun, MEMSHALAH, whose

---

[10] Ibn Ezra comments that the only thing that distinguishes the sun and the moon from the other celestial objects is the intensity of their light. He seems to think that all of these objects are in every other respect, including size, the same.

verbal root is mem (מ), shin (ש), lamed (ל). In the simple active conjugation the verb has two sets of radically different meanings. In some contexts, the verb is transitive, in which case it usually means "to rule" or "to govern" something. In other contexts, the verb is intransitive, in which case it usually means to make a comparison, to use a metaphor, and/or to speak in proverbs or parables. Hence, a noun derived from the verb could have, depending on context, the sense of some form of government and/or some kind of analogy.[11]

The noun formed from this verbal root, in all of its grammatical forms, occurs sixteen times in the Hebrew Scriptures,[12] but this is its only occurrence in the Pentateuch. Psalm 145:13 uses the terms, "MEMSHALAH" and "MALKHUT" as synonyms for a political state and/or kingdom. Similarly, Jeremiah uses these two words in conjunction. However, in his case there is a slight but significant difference in their meanings. In his usage, MEMSHALAH refers to the territory or territories over which the king's "hand," i.e., power, extends in a MALKHUT. As such the term, MEMSHALAH expresses a function, viz., the characteristic activity of a political state (MALKHUT), viz., governing, over a region of space. In other words, while both MALKHUT and MEMSHALAH have to do with the activity of governing, the former term applies to the institution of government while the latter applies to the spatial territory under government. The term, MEMSHALAH functions in the same way in First and Second Kings, Isaiah, Micah, Daniel, and Second Chronicles. In the case of the Psalms, this notion of the characteristic function of a political state is applied to the space of the entire universe. With specific reference to our narrative, Psalm 136:8-9 repeats this verse, and Psalm 103:22 commands everything made in every place under his MEMSHALAH, i.e., his political territory, to praise him. Similarly, Psalm 114:2 asserts that Israel is the territories subject to God's governance.

In sum, the primary sense of the noun "MAMSHELET" in our narrative is political rather than linguistic. It expresses a specific state-of-affairs relative to a specific territory of space. It says that the sun and

---

[11] For the sake of simplicity, I use the term, "analogy" as a general category of equivocal speech that includes "metaphor," "parable," and "proverb."
[12] Gen 1:16; 1 Kg. 9:19; 2 Kg 20:13; Isa 22:21; 39:2; Jer 34:1; 51:28; Micah 4:8; Ps 103:22; 114:2; 136:8,9; 145:13; Dan 11:5; 2 Chron 8:6; 32:9.

the moon have been made for the sake of affecting authority over the two primary regions of the sky, viz., day and night. The sun is commanded to act as a governor over the day, the moon is ordered to act as a governor over the night, and the entire space of the sky is conceived in terms of territories within a political state. In other words, the model of the divinely produced universe is understood first and foremost as something political. However, the linguistic sense of the verb, MASHAL, may not be entirely lacking in our narrative, since, after all, literally, the universe is not a kingdom, the sun and the moon are not governors, and God is not a king. This is another sense in which our narrative is a model, viz., its language is intentionally analogical.

Note that now our model functions in a significantly different way than it functioned in the description of the first three days. There, where the subject matter is space, the model is primarily a model for physics. Here, where the subject matter is the occupants of space, the model is primarily a model for politics.

ואת הכוכבים:
Ve-ET HA-KOKHAVIM
and the (other) celestial-objects.

All of the remaining lighters are referred to collectively as KOKHAVIM. The usual translation of this term is "stars," but that is not quite right. The term includes all of the objects located in the sky, both stars, viz., celestial objects that emit light, and celestial objects such as planets and asteroids that only reflect light. The term, "stars" is misleading, because it suggests that the author(s) of our text did not know this distinction, and our text provides no evidence one way or the other on this matter. In the *Genesis Rabbah* commentary on this verse, Rabbi Jochanan makes this distinction and Nachmanides and Sforno share his judgment. However, Rabbis Berekiah and Simon reject it, and both Rashi and Ibn Ezra agree with them. Note that all of these rabbis, including Nachmanides and Sforno, call both the light-emitting and the non-light-emitting celestial objects "KOKHAVIM."

Genesis 1:17

ויתן אתם אלהים ברקיע השמים להאיר על־הארץ:

VA-YITEN OTAM ELOHIM Be-RAKIYA' HA-SHAMAYIM Le-HA-IR 'AL-HA-ARETZ

God places them in the spread of the sky to enlighten the earth,

YITEN is a third person singular form of the imperfect tense in the Waw Consecutive of the simple active conjugation of the verb whose root is nun (נ), tet (ת), nun (נ). It is one of the more common verbs used in the Hebrew Scriptures, and it often occurs in this construction. It has a variety of meanings, which include "gives," "hands over," "grants," "yields," "allows," "permits," "lets," "puts," "establishes," "appoints," "makes," "renders," and "places." Within our context, the two most relevant senses are "to appoint or permit" and "to set or place." The former set has political connotations. In this sense the verb commonly is used when a governor makes an executive appointment or a judge rules that the law permits someone to do something. The latter set has spatial connotations. Both uses are intended here. God both positions the lighters in the space of the sky and he delegates to them, in virtue of their characteristic function and their location, authority to enlighten the surface of the earth. In this connection, it is of interest to note that the verb occurs only one more time in our narrative.[13] As the lighters are given authority and permission to enlighten the earth, so the human is given authority/permission to eat plants, fish, birds and animals.

Verse 17 seems to do nothing more than repeat what the narrative says in verse 15, viz., that the lighters be-come for the purpose of enlightening the circumference of the earth-filled central globe of the universe. However, there is a difference. Verse 15 is connected with verse 14. Together they deal with potentialities, a state-of-affairs, and a truth judgment. In contrast, verse 17 is connected with verses 16 and 18. Together they deal with the concomitant ideal, objects, and moral judgment.

Verse fourteen specifies the potential of the lighters to make it possible to distinguish different time periods from each other. This verse also singles out the division between day and night as a major mode of

---

[13] In Gen 1:29.

division that, in an as yet unspecified way, takes precedence over the other ways of reckoning time.¹⁴ Verse fifteen specifies the power that these objects possess that enables them to realize their potential. That power is the ability to enlighten space. Together, verses 14 and 15 make a truth judgment about a general state-of-affairs. The state is that the motion of lighters are to be understood as a continuous, goal directed function, whose limit or end is to use the alternation of light and dark in the sky in order to calculate time, whose purpose in turn is to separate time, just as the purpose of the spread is to separate space.¹⁵

In contrast, verses 16 through18 focus attention on the lighters themselves. Whereas the subject matter of verses 14 and 15 is a continuous event which contains objects, the subject-matter now shifts to the objects involved in the initial event. The event involves the acts of separating and enlightening. The actors who are the subjects of these verbs are the lighters. Verse 16 tells us that two of them, the sun and the moon, were made for a special political role, viz., to govern the primary division between day and night. Verse 17 tells us that all of the lighters exist for a special physical role, viz., to enlighten the earth. As we shall see, verse 18 will synthesize the two roles into a common ideal. Together these two verses form a model of a kind of polity whose citizens are lighters, governed by two of their compatriots. The polity is not an end in itself. Rather, it has a function that transcends both its collective self and its distributive members. That role is to enlighten.

The narrative's description of the dynamic event involves God saying something to be-come for the purpose of separating and enlightening. The narrative's description of the primary objects of the event involves God making some of them to govern and placing all of them to enlighten. Enlightening is involved in both cases. The difference is that God orders the event and makes the objects. However, once again, this does not mean that God performs two acts. Rather, these are different perspectives on a single, general fact. There are no actions without actors and no actors without actions. Neither the act or the

---

¹⁴ As we shall see below in the commentary on Gen 2:2-3, the excellence of the division of day and night over the other celestial time distinctions has to do with the special place of cosmic importance that our text assigns to the Sabbath.

¹⁵ God separates space. The question is, who separates time? The most obvious answer is, the as-yet-not-mentioned human being.

actor is primary. What is primary is the event that encompasses both. God produces the event. From one perspective, what God does is order actions. From another perspective, he makes actors. However, these are only perspectives.

Genesis 1:18

ולמשל ביום ובלילה ולהבדיל בין האור ובין החשך

Ve-LIMSHOL BA-YOM U-VA-LAYLAH UL-HAVDIL
BAYN HA-OR U-VAYN HA-CHOSHEKH

to govern the day and the night, and to separate the light from the dark,

The two clauses express the same state-of-affairs. "Day" is the name of the light, and "night" is the name of the dark. Similarly, the "governing" in this case at least is no different from the "separating." Where the "large lighter," viz., the sun, makes light, there is day. Where the other lighters make light, the space of the sky remains predominantly dark. Hence, where their ruler, viz., the moon, governs, there is night. In general, the narrative hints beyond this single event to the judgment that to rule is, to a great extent, to enforce a separation between opposites.

וירא אלהים כי־טוב:

VA-YAR ELOHIM KI-TOV

while God perceives that it is excellent.

This is the fourth object to be judged of value. First was the light of day one. Second and third were the seas/dry-land and vegetation of the third day. Fourth are the lighters of the fourth day.

The verbs used to express the fact that the lighters enlighten the earth closely parallel the verbs used to express the production of the lighters as ideal objects. In both cases the divine production involves enlightening (Le-HA-IR),[16] governing (LeMAMSHELET[17] and LIMSHOL[18]), and separating (Le-HAVDIL).[19] The difference is that

---

[16] Gen 1:14,17.
[17] Gen 1:16.
[18] Gen 1:18.
[19] Gen 1:14,18.

whereas God orders (YOMER)[20] and makes (YA'AS)[21] the fact, he places (YITEN)[22] the object. However, the difference is only a matter of perspective. There is only one event, viz., that the lighters have the ability to enlighten a specific region of space. That event involves a function that is intelligible in terms of its purpose. "Governing" and "separating" are activity terms that apply to the event from the perspective of its function. "Setting" is a stable state term with connotations of law and ethics (viz., permission). Neither the activity nor the state has reality independent of the other. What is real is the event.

Genesis 1:19

ויהי־ערב ויהי בקר יום רביעי:

VA-YeHIY-'EREV VA-YeHIY VOKER YOM ReVI'I

A fourth day there is evening and morning.

The first three days deal with the differentiation of space into different regions. The next three days deal with the differentiation of the occupants of that space.[23] As the light-stuff that differentiates the regions of day and night is the ideal product of the first day of space, so the lighters that govern this separation are the ideal product of the first day of spatial objects.

This phase of God godding the universe completes our text's description of space. We are told nothing about the differentiation of any

---

[20] Gen 1:14.

[21] Gen 1:16.

[22] Gen 1:17.

[23] The exception to this generalization is vegetation. *Prima facie* it is an occupant of space. However, it is a product of the third, rather than the fourth day. My guess is that the author(s) of our narrative does not really consider it to be an occupant. Rather, it is something transitional between space and occupant. In this sense, as we shall discuss below, it parallels the human being. As the last product of the generation of space is something more than a space but less than a spatial-occupant, the last product of the generation of objects, the human being, is something more than a spatial object. As vegetation is tied to but still transcends physical space, so the human is tied to but still transcends the other physical objects.

of the lighters into the regions of constellations and galaxies. The sole concern of our narrative with the regions of the universe beyond the globe of the planet earth is with the sun and the moon, which is sufficient to enable human beings to direct their religious festivals. As we shall see, it is the event of human worship of God that characterizes the ideal end of the entire universe.

Day 5

Genesis 1:20

ויאמר אלהים
VA-YOMER ELOHIM
God says,

This is God's sixth speech-act,[1] and the third time that God orders something to cause something else to come to be.[2] God speaks the light[3] and the sky[4] into existence, says that the lighters should separate day and night,[5] and orders the water to become collected[6] and the earth to sprout sprouts.[7] Now God orders the water to produce living occupants.

ישרצו המים שרץ
YISHReTZU HA-MAYIM SHERETZ
"Let the waters swarm a swarm

The water is given its second spoken command. On day three it is ordered to contract itself so that a separation can appear between the

---

[1] See Gen 1:3,6,9,11, 14.
[2] See Gen 1:9, 11.
[3] Gen 1:3.
[4] Gen 1:6.
[5] Gen 1:14.
[6] Gen 1:9.
[7] Gen 1:11-12.

surface of the earth and the seas.⁸ Here it is ordered to to generate something. As the earth on day three is ordered to DASHA DESHE (sprout a sprout),⁹ so the water here is ordered to SHARATZ a SHERETZ. As to sprout is the defining function of a sprout, so to SHARATZ is the defining function of a SHERETZ. As a sprout is what it does, viz., sprouts, so a SHERETZ is what it does, viz., SHARATZ. As the characteristic activity of a sprout refers both to its distinctive way of living and reproducing, so the characteristic activity of a SHERETZ refers both to its distinctive way of living and reproducing.

YISHReTZU is a third person, plural form in the imperfect tense of the simple active conjugation of the verb whose root is shin (ש), resh (ר), tsadik (צ). The verb means to "breed," "teem" and/or to "swarm," and/or to "multiply," "abound." The first two verbs refer to the act of reproducing. The next verb refers to the way these living products live. The last two verbs suggest that the act involves large numbers. In other words, what "swarms" gives birth to many offspring and lives together with large numbers of its own kind.

While the verb occurs many times in the Pentateuch, it occurs only twice in other parts of the Hebrew Scriptures.[10] While the use of this verb in our narrative is restricted to the activity of water, the verb also occurs when earth is the subject.[11]

The noun form of the verb, SHERETZ, is used generally to name a reptile or an insect. However, the reference is more general than this. For example, Leviticus 11 specifically mentions weasels, mice, lizards, geckos, crocodiles, and chameleons,[12] as well as locusts, crickets, and grasshoppers[13] under this heading, and this list is not intended to be all inclusive. What defines the category is the ease with which its members

---

[8] Gen 1:9-10.

[9] Gen 1:11-12.

[10] In Ps 105:30, where the land of the earth of Egypt is the subject and frogs are the object, and in Ez 47:9, where the water of rivers is the subject and fish are the object.

[11] E.g., Gen 7:21; 8:17; 9:7; Lev 11:29, 41-46.

[12] Lev 11:29-30, within the sub-category of SHERETZ that SHARATZ on the earth.

[13] Lev 11: 21-22, within the sub-category of SHERETZ that have wings, that leap about on earth with four legs.

can reproduce and the collective form of their existence. A "SHERETZ" is anything that swarms, i.e., that lives as part of a quantifiably large group and reproduces in large numbers, irrespective of where it resides (on the land, in the water, or in the sky) or what is its size (be it a microorganism, like a unicellular zoospore, or a complex macro-organism, like a bee).

The form of the verb is plural because the subject has a dual form, viz., the upper and lower waters. Critical here is the primacy of space over its occupants. That space is differentiated before spatial-objects does not mean that space exists before objects in a temporal sense. Rather, it indicates that space has ontological priority over its objects. It is not the case that objects merely are located in space; rather, space itself is what generates the objects. Similarly, it is not the case that space is characterized by what it contains; rather, space determines the characteristics of its occupants.

That the form of the verb is imperfect indicates that the activity is dynamic. As in the case of the water being told to collect itself together,[14] and the earth being told to sprout a sprout,[15] so here the verb is not joined to the consonant of conjunction. In these cases there is no sense that the activity has a limit, i.e., the capacity or power or potential for the water to congeal and for both the earth and the waters to generate large numbers of its occupants is infinite. In other words, the generation of physical things within the space of the universe is without beginning or end. This is another indication that the sense of origin in our narrative is not temporal. The universe as a whole is not subject to time. Time reigns within the universe, and its extent within its space is endless in both directions, viz., into the past as well as into the future.

נפש חיה
NEFESH CHAYAH
of fresh life

The noun, <u>CHAYAH</u> is formed from a verb whose root is chet (ח), yod (י), he (ה). The verb means "to live." Hence, a CHAYAH is an object whose characteristic act is to live, viz., a life.

---

[14] Gen 1:9.
[15] Gen 1:11.

The term NEFESH is formed from a verb whose root is nun (נ), pe (פ), shin (ש). The noun often is translated as "soul," but this translation is not correct. This English term presupposes a theory of being that makes a radical separation between what is physical/material and what is mental/spiritual, and this particular dualism does not fit any possible ontology in the Hebrew Scriptures. Similarly, the terms "mind" and "spirit" are common but erroneous translations of the noun, "NEFESH."

While the noun occurs frequently throughout the Hebrew Scriptures, the same cannot be said for the verb. It occurs only three times,[16] and in each of these cases, it is a third person, singular form of the imperfect tense in the simple passive conjugation, viz., YINAFESH. In 2 Samuel 16:14 we are told that David and his followers, in flight from Saul, were tired and "YINAFESH" there. Here, clearly the verb means to make a rest stop, i.e., to rest and become refreshed. In other words, the men were fresh, their labor made them cease to be fresh, and now, through rest, they once again (which is what the "re" in "refreshed" means) become fresh.

In Exodus 23:12 the verb is associated with the verbs for rest (HENIYACH) and for the characteristic form of activity (SHABAT) on the Sabbath. The seventh day is proclaimed a day on which you should SHABAT ("TISHBOT"), so that your livestock[17] will rest ("YANUACH") and your guests[18] will "YINAFESH," i.e., will regain their state of being fresh. Similarly, Exodus 31:17 joins YINAFESH to SHABAT. In this case the subject of the action is God. The context is an explanation of the work prohibitions on the Sabbath, with specific reference to the end of our narrative. We are told that, since God SHABATs and NAFASHes on the seventh day, Israel should observe the Sabbath by refraining from work.

Consequently, the noun, NEFESH describes something that is NAFASH, viz., is fresh. The term "fresh" is associated both with a living animal being active, i.e., being "lively," and with a dead animal being fit

---

[16] Viz., in Ex 23:12, 31:17, and 2 Sam 16:14.

[17] Literally, your ox and your ass.

[18] Literally, the son of your handmaid (AMATeKHA) and the resident-alien (GER), i.e., people who reside with you under your authority who are neither members of your family nor your possessions.

to eat, i.e., being "fresh meat."[19] Both senses of the term, fresh are appropriate here for two reasons. First, there is the immediate conjunction of the term "NEFESH" with "CHAYAH." Second, our narrative relates every living thing to man as food.[20]

The verb NAFASH in the simple active conjugation usually means to "rest," "recuperate," and "be refreshed," all of which are appropriate here, given the key role that the Sabbath plays in our narrative. However, most translations associate the noun, not with this usage of the verb, but with the way the term generally is used in the intensive active conjugation — viz., to "animate," "breathe life into," and "enliven" — even though this verb construction never occurs in the Hebrew Scriptures. They do so because of the association of the noun in this verse (and in verse 24) with the noun CHAYAH. In other words, these translations take the term NEFESH to describe what is distinctive about a CHAYAH, viz., that it is a form of animate life. However, the verb that expresses this distinctive characteristic is CHAYAH. For this purpose there is no need to add that a CHAYAH is a NEFESH. Hence, it is a better reading to say that the term NEFESH says something more about this entity than the fact that it lives, viz., that it is the kind of living thing that has a capacity to rest and to become refreshed,[21] and, as such, it has a capacity to do whatever it means to perform the characteristic activity of the seventh day.

ועוף יעופף על־הארץ על־פני רקיע השמים:
Ve-'OF Ye'OFEF 'AL-HA-ARETZ 'AL-PeNAI RAKIYA' HA-SHAMAYIM
(that includes) a flier that flies above the earth throughout the spread of the sky."

The sprout that the earth produces is of two kinds — a plant ('ESEV) that either does or does not bear fruit (PeRI). Similarly, the

---

[19] "Meat" is what an animal becomes when it is killed for food. Immediately after being killed, it is fresh. However, the longer it remains dead, the less fresh it becomes. (For example, the sign above a butcher shop proclaiming "fresh killed meat" means that the meat in the store comes from animals recently killed.) Hence, the source of meat being fresh is the life of the animal. An animal's "freshness" is the last characteristic it loses when it no longer is alive.
[20] Gen 1:29-30.
[21] I.e., to again become fresh, i.e., to become re-fresh.

swarm that the waters produce is of two kinds — a fresh life (NEFESH CHAYAH) that does or does not Ye'OFEF. The fruit bearing object is called a "tree" ('ETZ), but it is understood that a tree is a kind of plant. Similarly, the swarm that YE'OFEF is called an "'OF," but it is understood that an 'OF is a kind of swarm.

An 'OF is that kind of fresh life swarm that flies over the surface of the planet earth — both the dry-land and the seas — through the spread-stuff that fills the space of the sky. Like every other fresh life that the water generates, it swarms, i.e., it can reproduce in prolific numbers and its offspring live in large collectives of their own species. They differ from other water-produced-swarming-fresh-life by their capacity to fly within the sky above the surface of the earth.

The ability to fly may be the sole distinguishing characteristic between these two kinds of swarming fresh life. However, there may be one additional distinction. The form of the term MAYIM is dual but its meaning could be singular as well as dual. Where the referent is the element, water, clearly the meaning is singular. However, where the referent is to space, after the second day the meaning can be dual, viz., a reference to both the upper and the lower waters. That is the sense in which I read the subject in this verse, i.e., swarming fresh life is generated by the upper and the lower waters. Now, given that these living things are of two kinds, it may be the case that the lower waters generate all of the forms that do not fly, (e.g., the fish), while the upper waters generate all of the forms that fly (e.g., the birds).

Whether or not an 'OF is a bird depends on your definition of a bird. Once again, an "'OF" is defined by its ability to swarm and to fly. Given that the characteristics that define the term "bird" are being warm-blooded, having feathers, laying eggs, being a vertebrate, and having wings as fore limbs, then some species of "bird" are not an 'OF (e.g., a dodo and most domestic turkeys and chickens, because they cannot fly, or a bald-eagle, because it does not swarm), and some species of "'OF" are not birds (e.g., a pterodactyl).[22]

---

[22] The same can be said about the term, "fish." Given that a fish is a cold-blooded craniate vertebrate with permanent gills that belongs to the class of Pisces in the phylum Chordate, then not every swarming fresh life generated by the lower water is a fish (e.g., a whale).

The region of flight is the sky. As we have already seen,[23] "'AL-PeNAI" means "at every dimension of," i.e., "throughout." In this respect, "sky" (SHAMAYIM) can be defined as the space that exclusively determines flight, and "spread" (RAKIYA') can be defined as the kind of stuff in which flight can occur. The space and stuff of water could be defined in an analogous manner in terms of the act of swimming. Conversely, the space and stuff of earth could be defined in terms of not admitting either activity. However, our narrative does not do so. Space is defined by its stuff, and not by what its occupants can do. As we shall see, only the seventh day, which determines time rather than space, is defined this way. Hence, our narrative makes a radical distinction between space and time as dimensions of the universe. Space is primary in the sense of origin; but, as we shall see,[24] time is primary in the sense of end (*telos*).

Genesis 1:21

ויברא אלהים
VA-YIVRA ELOHIM
God gods

YIVRA is a third person, singular form in the imperfect tense, joined to the consonant of conjunction, in the simple, active conjugation of the verb whose root is bet (ב), resh (ר), aleph (א). This is the first use of the verb within the narrative itself. In its sole earlier appearance,[25] it is a third person, singular form in the perfect tense in the simple, active conjugation. There it expresses the stable state of what God does in general within the single event that our narrative describes. Here it designates one aspect of that event, viz., what God does on the fifth day, as a dynamic state that is directed towards a stable end. On the second day, when God orders the spread to be-come, he "makes" it.[26] Similarly, on the fourth day, when he orders the lighters to become, he "makes"

---

[23] Gen 1:2.
[24] In connection with the seventh day.
[25] In Gen 1:1.
[26] Gen 1:6-7.

them.[27] In both cases only a single action is described, i.e., the ordering and the making are the same thing. Furthermore, when God orders the lighters, he makes the sun, the moon, and the celestial-objects. The objects of the making are three sub-species of the ordering. "Lighters" is a general term, while "the large lighter" (viz., the sun) and "the small lighter" (viz., the moon) are individual objects. "Celestial-objects" is also a general term, but more restricted than "lighters," viz., it delineates the class of all lighters excluding the sun and the moon. In this respect, the description of the fifth day parallels that of the fourth day. The swarm of fresh life ordered into existence in verse 20 is referred to here in three sub-species, and the verbs in both verses express the same relation between God and his product. In other words, the expression, "God gods" in this verse means what the waters generate in response to God's command. The actions of both God and the waters are part of God's godding.

This usage illuminates two respects in which God godding the universe is unlike anyone else creating anything. First, creators usually do not create solely by speaking. Second, while artisans make artifacts with tools, as God makes the universe with space, the ones who actually make the artifacts are the artisans, not their tools. In contrast, here it is space, not God, that takes the actual direct action. What is closer to God godding the universe than artists creating works of art are rulers ruling states. As the rulers's proclamations to subjects produce political reality, so God's speech to space produces physical reality. Hence, the verb "governs" (MASHAL) comes closer to what it is that God is doing in our narrative than the verb "makes" ('ASAH). The image here is one of a single governor at the head of a carefully defined social-political-administrative pyramid. On this model, God is the monarch (or C.E.O.), while the lighters and the regions of space are his first ministers (or, executive officers), and the universe is the political state (or, corporation).

---

[27] Gen 1:14-16.

את־התנינם הגדלים
ET-HA-TeNINIM HA-GeDOLIM
the large sea-serpents,

TeNINIM is the masculine plural form of a noun whose singular form is TANIN. It often means a variety of wild land animals, reptiles (such as crocodiles dragons and/or serpents), and/or unusually large/mysterious sea creatures (such as whales and/or sea-monsters). It is not certain what the root is. The most likely candidate is taf(ת), nun (נ), nun (נ), in which case the closest candidate for a verbal source of the noun's meaning is TINYAN. However, this verb, which means to sing or play the second part of a piece of music, does not appear in the Hebrew Scriptures.[28] The noun appears four more times in the Pentateuch — once in Deuteronomy[29] in the plural, and three times in the same passage of Exodus[30] in the singular. In Deuteronomy, the word is a general term for snakes; in Exodus it names what Moses and Aaron transform Aaron's staff into, in order to demonstrate God's power to Pharoah and the Egyptians. This use of the term also occurs in Psalm 91:13. This would suggest "snakes" as the most likely translation of the term here. However, most modern translators prefer "sea-monsters," and both Rashi and the sages of *Genesis Rabbah* take the term to have a singular reference to the mythical sea-monster, Leviathan.

The singular form of the noun appears nine more times,[31] and the plural thirteen more times,[32] in the rest of the Hebrew Scriptures. It is used only once[33] to mean Leviathan, only three times to mean a sea-monster,[34] and only four times to mean a dragon.[35] In fact, the most frequent use of the term is to refer to some kind of wild land animal, such

---

[28] I do not know the origin of the verb. It may be strictly a creation of modern Hebrew.

[29] In 32:33.

[30] In 7:9,10,12.

[31] In Isa 27:1; 51:9; Jer 51:34; Ez 29:3; 32:2; Ps 91:13; 74:13; 148:7; and Job 7:12.

[32] In Isa 13:22; 34:13; 35:7; 43:20; Jer 9:10; 10:22; 14:6; 49:33; 51:37; Micah 1:8; Ps 44:20; Job 30:29; Lam 4:3.

[33] In Isa 27:1.

[34] In Ps 74:13; 148:7; Job 7:12.

[35] In Isa 51:9; Jer 51:34; Ez 29:3; 32:2.

as a wild dog, jackal and/or ass. The term has this meaning in thirteen disparate places in the Hebrew Scriptures.[36] If frequency of use were the arbiter, the likely translation would be "wild-animals." However, the context makes it clear that this is not what the term means here. Whatever TeNINIM are, they are wild, but they are not land animals. Clearly, they are a specific sub-category of swarming fresh life, that is generated by the water, and is distinguished from the other members of this species by its size. For this reason, sea-serpents is a likely interpretation, i.e., large, wild snakes that reside in the water.

ואת כל-נפש החיה הרמשת אשר שרצו המים למינהם
Ve-ET KOL-NEFESH HA-CHAYAH HA-ROMESET
ASHER SHARTZU HA-MAYIM Le-MINAIHEM
every creeping fresh life that the waters swarm according to their own kind,

This phrase parallels the term "celestial-objects," in the previous verse. There the lighters are divided into three sub-groups, two specific objects (the sun and the moon) and the class of all lighters excluding the sun and the moon. Similarly, this phrase designates the general class of swarming fresh life produced by water, excluding sea serpents and the fliers with wings mentioned in the next phrase. The distinguishing characteristic of this sub-category is its members' ability to "ROMESET."

ROMESET is a feminine singular participle in the simple active conjugation of the verb whose root is resh (ר), mem (מ), sin (ש). There are multiple appearances of the verb in several constructions in the Hebrew Scriptures. The noun formed from the verb (REMES) usually means anything that creeps — rather than walks, flies or swims — irrespective of its size or where it resides, i.e., a creeper. In fact the most common examples of creeping things reside on land, viz., maggots, insects, worms, and serpents. However, our context restricts the range here solely to water-based creepers. Land-based creepers will be noted in verse 24.

Since the sea-serpents of the first clause (because they are serpents) also are creepers, size probably determines the members of this class. This is another respect in which the sub-classification of fresh life

---

[36] In Isa 13:22; 34:13; 35:7; 43:20; Jer 9:10; 10:22; 14:6; 49:33; 51:37; Micah 1:8; Ps 44:20; Job 30: 29; Lam 4:3.

parallels the sub-classification of lighters. As the two lighters (viz., the sun and the moon) are exempted from the general class of lighters because of their size (viz., they are larger than the other members of the grouping), so here too the sea-serpents simply are creepers whose distinguishing characteristic is their exceptional size in comparison to the other general members of the class. It is interesting to note that, in both cases, a quantitative difference (viz., size), when sufficiently great, can constitute a qualitative difference (viz., definition).

ואת כל־עוף כנף למינהו
Ve-ET KOL-'OF KHANAF Le-MINAIHU
and every winged flier according to its own kind,

The distinguishing characteristic of this general sub-category of fresh-life-swarms is that they have wings with which to fly through the spread of the sky. As such, this is a category whose level is comparable to the creepers. Whether or not the sea-serpents can fly as well is an open question. Our text says nothing about it. It could be the case, in parallel to the specification of the types of lighters, that the sea-generated, swarming fresh life can creep or fly, so that sea-serpents are exceptionally large examples of the general category, which includes both creeping and flying varieties. Again, it is not clear whether the water is commanded to generate anything that can do both, and, if it can, into what category such swarms fall.

While it is clear that not all fliers are birds, it is not clear whether our text (despite the erroneous ornithology) considers all birds to be fliers. The most likely textual answer is yes. As we shall see, the earth is ordered on the sixth day to generate its own varieties of fresh life. In this case, the forms include creepers, but neither swarms nor fliers. This omission suggests that the author(s) of our narrative believes that every kind of physical object that swarms or flies, irregardless of where it resides, is generated by water. Hence, the primary basis of the classification of the occupants of space is their spatial origin, and there is no necessary correlation between the source of the occupant and where it resides. Hence, swarms of fliers, such as bees and gnats, who reside on land, are here said to have their origin in the space and stuff of water.

וירא אלהים כי־טוב:
VA-YAR ELOHIM KI-TOV
while God perceives that it is excellent.

This is the fifth object that God judges to be of value. In terms of the differentiation of space, he makes this judgment about light (day 1), and the land/seas (day 3). In terms of the generation of the occupants of space, he makes this judgment about vegetation (day 3) and lighters (day 4). Now, on day 5, he also judges the product of water to be excellent. Note that this is a moral/end judgment rather than a truth/function judgment. In every case it is not the products that are generated. Rather, the product is a generative capacity with which space is endowed. The light judged excellent on day one has the power to enlighten, but it does not do so until the fourth day when there are lighters. Similarly here on the fifth day, what is judged excellent is the actual power of the water to generate swarms. However, as of yet no swarms have been generated.

Genesis 1:22

ויברך אתם אלהים לאמר
VA-YeVAREKH OTAM ELOHIM LAIMOR
God blesses them by saying,

<u>VA-YeVAREKH</u>: This is the first of three appearances[37] in our narrative of the verb whose root in bet (ב), resh (ר), kaph (כ). In every case it has this construction, viz., a third person, singular form in the imperfect tense of the intensive active conjugation, joined to the consonant of conjunction. As such, the verb expresses the stable end-state of what is a dynamic process. In this (and the next) case, the verb is a direct action verb whose subject is God, and whose objects are what God gods. In the simple active conjugation the verb has something to do with kneeling. In the intensive active construction it generally means, "to bless." The blessing is followed by <u>LAIMOR</u>, i.e., by saying something. The something is a set of imperatives concerning those blessed. Hence,

---

[37] Gen 1:22, 28; 2:3. The subject/actor in all three cases is God. The objects/recipients-of-the-action are, respectively, sea-generated fresh-life-swarms, the human, and the Sabbath.

prima facie the "saying" is "commanding." Here, on the fifth day, the objects (i.e., the "them," OTAM) that God gods/blesses/commands are all of the fresh life that the waters swarm. On the sixth day the object godded/blessed/commanded is the human.[38]

To "be blessed" generally means to receive something unusual, of special value, that will bring special happiness, good fortune, prosperity, and/or protection to the recipient. In this sense, that one thing is blessed and another is not entails that the former is singled out in a way that favors it over the latter. Hence, the sea generated swarm of fresh life, in some special way, has an advantage over everything else not so fortunate. The advantage seems to be that both the human and the sea swarm are godded and are the object of commandments.

All of the classical rabbinic commentators identify the blessing with the subsequent set of imperatives. On their reading, the apparent commandments are not obligations; rather, they are predictions, i.e., the text says that these swarms *will* be fruitful and multiply, and these fliers *will* fly; it is not the case that they *ought* to do so. Hence, the blessing is that reproduction is something that these swarms (in opposition to every other form of fresh life) can perform without effort. In other words, what uniquely distinguishes the sea swarms is the ease with which they can generate, and thereby preserve and prosper, their species. Similarly, fliers are uniquely blessed by their ability to fly, which eases their own instinctual efforts to preserve and prosper their species.[39] I would agree with this interpretation in only one respect, viz., that the recipients of this command, i.e., what becomes obligated to act in a certain way, are not the fresh life forms generated by the waters.

---

[38] Gen 1:27-28.

[39] Given this interpretation, Rashi reasons that the land animals should have been separated out from the others for a special blessing of procreation. Because humans will eat the fresh life of the land more than sea life, land life is the most endangered species. However, Rashi explains, they did not receive the additional blessing, viz., an increased capacity to reproduce naturally, because of the sin of the serpent in the Garden of Eden.

פרו ורבו ומלאו את־המים בימים והעוף ירב בארץ:

PeRU U-RVU U-MIL-U ET-HA-MAYIM BA-YAMIM Ve-HA-'OF YIREV BA-ARETZ

"Be fruitful, increase, and fill the water in the seas, but the flier is to increase on the land."

The commandment consists of three plural imperatives — PeRU, RVU, and MIL-U. PeRU is formed from the root pe (פ), resh (ר), he (ה). The noun, "PeRI" (fruit), that is the object that the "'ETZ" (tree plant) is said to "make,"[40] has the same root. The verb can mean to "be fertile," "produce children," "reproduce," and/or "grow," "produce," "thrive" and/or "be fruitful." The first three translations clearly state the primary sense of the verb, viz., to generate offspring of the same kind. The next three translations have a broader, less physical, sense of succeeding at an activity.[41] The last expression, "be fruitful," preserves the ambiguity of both sets of meanings, with the added advantage of suggesting the noun formed from the verb.

RVU is formed from the root resh (ר), bet (ב), he (ה). It can mean to "multiply," "increase," "grow," and/or to be-come "large", "great," "much." In the sense of "grow," the term is a synonym for "PeRU," and, in all probability, this is its intent in our text. However, the other English translations of the term add a dimension to its meaning that differs from the connotations of the first verb. Whereas "PeRU" is primarily associated with generation, "RVU" is primarily associated with excessive, quantifiable size (viz., "large" and "great") as well as the mathematical function of multiplication. The English term that best retains all of these senses of the Hebrew is "increase."

MIL-U is formed from the root mem (מ), lamed (ל), aleph (א). Whereas the first two verbs are imperative forms of the simple, active conjugation, this imperative is a form of the intensive active conjugation. The verb means to be-come full. The imperative suggests that its recipient is ful-filled when its space is filled. Hence, the conjunction of these three verbs together suggests a single command, viz., that the sea

---

[40] Gen 1:12.
[41] For example, an investment can "grow," an experiment can "produce" a result, and a business can "thrive."

generated swarm should bear fruit and increase until they completely fill up their designated region of space.

YIREV is a shortened form of the third person, singular in the imperfect tense of the simple active conjugation of the verb whose root is resh (ר), bet (ב), he (ה). This is the same verb that appears as the second imperative (RVU) in the command imposed upon the waters. As such, it is not a fourth aspect of the command. Rather, it is a modification of the single imperative. Whereas the commandment is that the swarm should increase until the space of the waters is entirely (ful-)filled with this swarm, the fliers will increase on the surface of the land.

The three-imperative conjunction (viz., be fruitful, increase and fill) only occurs four times in the Hebrew Scriptures. In each case the commander is God. In this instance, the object of the command is the sea generated swarm. Next, the original human will be the object,[42] and then (in two separate verses within the same narrative) Noah and his descendents.[43] The general assumption is that these objects also are the recipients of the commandment. In other words, the command does not merely deal with the objects; the objects are what are commanded. However, at least in the case of the swarm, this interpretation is not obvious. Consider the following example: Abraham commands Isaac to teach Jacob to walk. In this case, the object of the command is Jacob walking; however, Jacob is not the recipient of the command. Rather, Isaac is, i.e., it is Isaac, not Jacob, who bears the obligation to cause something to happen. Now, the commandment in this verse has the same form, i.e., the waters are like Isaac, and the swarms are like Jacob. In other words, it is not the case that the swarm is commanded to be-fruitful/increase/fill. Rather, it is the waters that are commanded to generate something, viz., the varieties that the waters swarm. So understood, generation is an asymptotic function whose origin is a region of space filled solely with water-stuff, and whose end is that same region filled with fresh life. In this case it is the space that transforms itself from having one kind of character (viz., being filled with elementary water) to having another kind of character (viz., being filled

---

[42] Gen 1:28.

[43] Gen 9:1. In Gen 9:7 they are commanded again in slightly different language. Here they are told to PeRU and RVU as well as to SHIRTZU (swarm) and RVU on the earth.

with fresh life), where the life forms are to be understood, not as distinct substances that occupy space but, as modifications of the space itself.[44]

Genesis 1:23

ויהי-ערב ויהי בקר יום חמישי:
VA-YeHIY-'EREV VA-YeHIY VOKER YOM CHAMISHI
A fifth day there is evening and morning.

On day one, God orders the light to appear, in order to distinguish between light and dark, in order to name the day and the night. On the second day, God verbally makes the spread, in order to distinguish between the upper and lower waters, in order to name the sky. On the third day, God completes the differentiation of space and begins the generation of its occupants. He orders the waters to congeal so that the dry land may appear, so that he can name earth and seas. In addition, he orders the earth to sprout a sprout of plant that does and does not bear fruit. On the fourth day, God produces the lighters that occupy the sky. He verbally makes the lighters and places them in the sky, in order both to distinguish between the light and the dark and to govern day and night, in order to enlighten the surface of the earth. Now, on the fifth day, God gods the fresh life swarms that occupy the waters. He blesses the waters with a commandment to swarm fertile fresh life creepers that do and do not fly, in order to (ful)fill its space. First, the space of the universe is differentiated into regions. Second, each region is differentiated by a distinctive generating function through which it becomes characterized by an infinite sequence of reproducing occupants. Having made sky and

---

[44] Although this is no place for such an argument, I would claim that something like this ontology is what Spinoza intended to communicate in *The Ethics* through his definition and use of the terms "substance," "attribute," and "mode." "Substance" is the space of the universe. The "modes" are not themselves substances; rather, they are differentiations within the single entity, substance. Finally, "attributes" are different ways of viewing the single reality that is space. One way to view that substantive reality is as "extension," i.e., physical space. Another way to view it is as "mind," i.e., as mental/spiritual space. However, the space itself (like the universe of our narrative), in reality, is neither.

distinguished earth and water, God commands space to generate occupants. Having ordered the occupants of the sky and the waters, what remains to be commanded are the fertile occupants of the earth. This task is the work of the sixth day.

Day 6

Genesis 1:24

ויאמר אלהים תוצא הארץ נפש חיה למינה
VA-YOMER ELOHIM TOTZE HA-ARETZ NEFESH CHAYAH Le-MINAH
God says, "Let the earth produce fresh life of its own kind

This is the second instance in our narrative of the earth producing (TOTZE) something. On the third day the product is vegetation, i.e., a sprout that can either bear or not bear fruit.[1] There what is produced is not individual plants. Rather, the product is a single prototype within which is a capacity or disposition to produce an endless variety of distinctive, particular plants at different times at every place on earth. Properly speaking, the verse describes God empowering the earth with the ability to produce. Nothing actually is produced. The same is true of the events described on both the fifth and the sixth days. We are told nothing about the chronology of living things. Once again, our narrative is an atemporal model for understanding the universe; it is not the first event in its temporal history.

The work of the sixth day parallels the work of the fifth day. There God says that the waters should swarm their kind of fresh life. Here God says that the earth should produce its kind of fresh life. In both cases the source of generation is God's speech-act (YOMER), and what is generated is fresh life. On the fifth day the proximate cause of living things is the characteristic act of the waters, viz., swarming

---

[1] Gen 1:12.

(YISHRETZU) things.² Here, on the sixth day, the proximate cause of living things is the characteristic act of the earth, viz., producing things.

First, God gods the varieties of space. They are earth, sky, and the two regions of water. All that distinguishes the two water regions are their location — one above and the other below the sky. In every other respect they are the same, i.e., they are composed of the same primary stuff, viz., water. Then, God gods the varieties of spatial occupants on the next three days. They are vegetation, lighters, and two kinds of fresh life.³

What distinguishes the two forms of life is their origin — waters for the one and earth for the other. How they differ is that one is swarmed, and the other is produced. However, this difference is not a matter of the nature of the products themselves. In fact, there are instances in the Hebrew Scriptures where things other than the earth "produce,"⁴ and not everything that "swarms" originates from the waters.⁵ Furthermore, our narrative already has stated that, while the waters produce fliers, fliers reside on the earth.⁶ Rather, the difference has to do with how the space and stuff of water differs from the space and stuff of earth. In general, differences in objects are due to their dispositions, and dispositions are determined by the space from which the objects originate.

---

² Gen 1:20.

³ Note that, while our narrative distinguishes vegetation and lighters (together with fresh life) from either the regions or stuff of space, it does not consider them to be living things. In contrast, we consider vegetation, but not lighters, to be alive. Most medieval astronomers/scientists/philosophers/theologians considered both to be alive. This is evident from the fact that they assigned appropriate souls to both vegetation and the celestial spheres. The souls of the spheres, often called "separate intellects," were identified with the angels.

⁴ For example, in Ruth 2: 18 Ruth produces (TOTZE) an ephah of barley for her mother-in-law.

⁵ For example, in Gen 8:17 God tells Noah that all life, including all of the forms that are produced on the sixth day of our narrative, should swarm on the earth (SHARTZU VA-ARETZ).

⁶ Gen 1:22.

Day 6

בהמה ורמש וחיתו־ארץ למינה
BeHEMAH VA-REMES Ve-CHAYTO-ARETZ Le-MINAH
(that includes) domestic animal, creeper and wild animal of its own kind,"

Both vegetation (DESHE) and swarm (SHERETZ) were differentiated into two first-level categories — plant and fruit tree for the vegetation, and fresh life and flier for the swarm. The fresh life is further classified into two second-level categories — life whose origin is the water, and life whose origin is the earth. Both of these second-level categories are further classified into three third-level categories. For water-originated life it is large sea-serpents, a creeper, and a winged-flier. For earth-originated life it is a BeHEMAH, a REMES, and a CHAYTO-ARETZ.

A <u>REMES</u>, as we have seen before,[7] is a creeper, i.e., something whose characteristic activity is creeping — as opposed to walking, flying or swimming. In this case the intended creepers are land-creepers, in opposition to all of the other earth-originating fresh life that walk upon the land. In general, I will adopt the convention of using the term, "animal" to refer to all earth-originating fresh life that are not creepers, i.e., that are either a BeHEMAH or a CHAYTO-ARETZ.

The term, <u>BeHEMAH</u> is a feminine, singular noun whose verbal root is bet (ב), he (ה), mem (מ). While the verb never appears in the Hebrew Scriptures, the use of the noun is frequent. In the intensive active and the reflective conjugations, the verb is associated with acting/being-acted-upon like a brute or a beast. Hence, the verb would suggest that this term in our narrative names that kind of land animal that acts like a brute or a beast, i.e., a wild animal. However, the most common referent in the Hebrew Scriptures for this general term are cattle, which suggests just the opposite meaning, viz., that a "BeHEMAH" is a domestic animal, i.e., something that is like 'a beast of burden.'

A <u>CHAYTO-ARETZ</u> would seem to be the most general of the three terms. The second word (ARETZ) simply means "earth." The first word, "CHAYTO," is a feminine, singular form of the noun for "life" (CHAYAH) with a third person, singular, masculine possessive pronoun as a suffix. The simplest interpretation is that the pronoun refers to the

---

[7] Gen 1:21.

noun, viz., the "its" of "its life" refers to this life itself.[8] In that case, the expression literally means something that "its life [CHAYTO] (is of/to/from/by) earth [ARETZ]." Like the "celestial-objects" (KOKHAVIM), which are every kind of lighter that is not the sun or the moon, and like "every fresh life creeper that the waters swarm",[9] which includes every kind of sea-swarm that is not a large sea-serpent or a winged-flier, so a "CHAYTO-ARETZ" is any kind of earth-produced fresh life that is not a creeper or a domestic animal. Hence, by elimination, a "CHAYTO-ARETZ" is a wild animal.[10]

Note that while the creeper (and everything else that we have discussed so far) is defined by what it does (viz., creep), animals are not differentiated by what they do, but by how they relate to human beings. One is something that humans can use (viz., domestic animals), while the other in general is something that threatens them (viz., wild animals). In other words, as the day/light and night/dark of the day one is not anything until the lighters are introduced on the fourth day, so the animals of the first half of the sixth day are not anything until the human is introduced in the second half of the day.

Furthermore, note that with only four exceptions (the seas,[11] the lighters, celestial-objects, and the sea-serpents), everything generated is in the singular. God gods a light and dark, a day and night, a spread, a sky, an earth and dry land, a sprout, a plant, a fruit-tree, a swarm, a fresh life, a flier, here a BeHEMAH, a REMES, and a CHAYTO-ARETZ, and next the human and the Sabbath. The use of the singular in all of these cases is further textual evidence that what God gods in our narrative is not our actual, infinitely individuated/particularized universe. Rather, it is a model for understanding the actual world, where the model speaks only about prototypes for each general species

---

[8] What is problematic here is that the pronoun and the noun are of different genders. An alternative translation would be "his life," i.e., a land-originated life form where the life belongs to God.

[9] Gen 1:21.

[10] This interpretation agrees with Ibn Ezra's commentary. Nachmanides says that the BeHEMAH is an animal that eats plants and a CHAYTO-ARETZ is a carnivorous animal.

[11] With MAYIM you cannot tell. The form is dual for both the singular (water) and the plural (waters).

of thing in the universe, and these paradigms are to be understood as permanent dispositions within space itself. If anything in the model is actual, it is space. Everything else is only a dispositional property of the space.

וַיְהִי־כֵן:
VA-YeHIY-KHEN
and it becomes so.

This is the fifth, and penultimate, dynamic state-of-affairs to be judged true. It is the case that the spread separates the upper and lower waters,[12] and separates the dry land and the seas.[13] It is also the case that the earth produces vegetation,[14] and the lighters enlighten the earth.[15] *Prima facie* we are told here that it is the case that the earth produces fresh life. However, this interpretation is problematic, for there is no apparent reason why verse 20 does not also say, after God orders the water to swarm a swarm, "and it becomes so." A more coherent interpretation of our narrative would be that the entire act of empowering space (both the waters and the earth) to generate fresh life is a single event. Hence, what "becomes so" is the function of reproduction, i.e., the space-determined capacity of all fresh life to be fertile.

Genesis 1:25

וַיַּעַשׂ אֱלֹהִים אֶת־חַיַּת הָאָרֶץ לְמִינָהּ וְאֶת־הַבְּהֵמָה לְמִינָהּ
VA-YA'AS ELOHIM ET-CHAYAT HA-ARETZ
Le-MINAH Ve-ET-HA-BeHEMAH Le-MINAH
God makes wild animal according to its kind, domestic animal according to its kind,

On the fifth day, God telling the water to swarm its fresh life is followed by God godding its three subdivisions. Similarly, on the sixth

---

[12] Gen 1:7 on day 2.
[13] Gen 1:9 on day 3.
[14] Gen 1:11, also on day 3.
[15] Gen 1:15 on day 4.

day, God telling the earth to produce its fresh life is followed by God making (YA'AS) its three subdivisions. The "godding" of water-originating fresh life is the same as the "making" of earth-originating fresh life.

In verse 24, the order of reference is domestic animal, creeper, and wild animal. Here the order is wild animal, domestic animal, and creeper. This arrangement makes more sense than the previous one. Wild and domestic animals should go together simply because they are both animals and they are distinguished by the way they relate to humans, viz., as a danger in the former case and as something of use/value in the latter case.

In the previous verse the wild animal is called a "CHAYTO-ARETZ," viz., something that "its life is of/to/from/by earth." Here it is called a "CHAYAT HA-ARETZ," viz., "a life (of/to/from/by) the earth." The referent in both cases is the same. I do not think that the facts that in the first case there is a possessive pronoun suffix added to "life," and that there is the definite article (HA) prefixed to "earth" in the second case, changes the meaning. In fact, for reasons already discussed,[16] the token in this verse is the preferred reference for a wild animal, viz., a "life of the earth" that is not domestic and is not a "creeper."

ואת כל-רמש האדמה למינהו
Ve-ET KOL-REMES HA-ADAMAH Le-MINAIHU
and every creeper of the humus according to its kind,

In the previous verse the creeper is simply called a "creeper" (REMES). However, there are two kinds of creepers, viz., those that the waters swarm,[17] and those whose origin is the earth. Here we are told that the latter is "KOL-REMES HA-ADAMAH."

"KOL" is a general term for "every" that is used in both a collective sense (i.e., "all," taken together to refer to a group) and a distributive sense (i.e., "any," taken to refer to each member of a group individually). Whether either or both senses of the term is intended in this context is not self-evident. Based on what was explained above

---

[16] Gen 1:24.
[17] Gen 1:21.

about the occupants of space being paradigms,[18] I would think that both senses are intended. What is created is a single individual that is the prototype of every member of the class.

Where the prototype (and its consequent class members) creep (REMES) is at, near, upon, and/or in the "ADAMAH." ADAMAH is a feminine singular noun whose verbal root is aleph (א), daled (ד), mem (מ). The root appears in the Hebrew Scriptures ten times as a verb,[19] sixteen times as an adjective,[20] and many times as either a masculine or a feminine noun. The adjective means red, and the verb is used to say that something is red or that it makes something else red. By extension the verb can also mean to blush (viz., turn red), insult, and/or shame (viz., cause someone to turn red). One of the noun forms of this root are "ADOM," which can mean the color red and/or redness, and, by extension, a blush, a flush, rouge, or a red jewel such as a ruby. The feminine noun based on this root in our text can mean "soil," "land," "earth," "ground," "territory," and/or a "country."

Given the etymology of the noun, I imagine that the soil of the people who coined the word was something like the red clay of Louisiana. As such the meaning of the "ADAMAH" here is close to the meaning of the "YAVASHAH" (dry land) in verse 9. In fact it could be a synonym, introduced here only in order to prepare us for the masculine counterpart of the term ("ADAM," human being) in the next verse. As such, "ADAMAH" could be translated simply as "land." However, one disadvantage of this translation is that the term lacks any association with what is red. In fact, if etymology were the arbiter, the translation should be "redland," "clay," or "soil." All three words designate something that is mostly earth but also is determined by the element water, since each English term conveys a different kind of mixture of these two more basic materials. However, the context makes it clear that what is meant by the term is the surface of the dry land, and not the surface of the earth that is below the seas. In other words, the "creeper" that the waters swarm creeps beneath the seas at its earth surface, while

---

[18] In connection with Gen 1:11-13 and 24.
[19] Ex 25:5; 35:7,23; 26:14; 36:19; 39:34; Isa 1:18; Nah 2:4; Prov 23:31; Lam 4:7.
[20] Gen 25:25,30; Lev 13:19, 24, 42, 43, 49; 14:37; Nu 19:2; 1 Sam 16:12;17:42; 2 Kgs 3:22; Isa 63:2; Zach 1:8; 6:2; Song of Songs 5:10.

the "creeper of the ADAMAH" creeps beneath the sky at its earth surface.

No English term seems capable of capturing all the subtleties of "ADAMAH." The word "ground" comes close, since it can mean "soil" and/or "land." "Ground" has the advantage of having a more general meaning than "soil," and it avoids the misleading linguistic association of "land" with the English translation of YAVASHAH as "dry land." However, the major weakness of all of these English terms is that they fail to reveal the text's connection of "ADAMAH" with the Hebrew term, "ADAM" in the next verse for the human. Given the importance of this relationship in our text, there are two possible routes open for translation, viz., either to use a standard English translation for "ADAMAH" and let that dictate how to translate "ADAM," or to do the opposite. On the former alternative, if "ADAMAH" is translated as "ground" or "soil," then "ADAM" could be translated as "grounder" or "soiler," viz., as an occupant formed from ground/soil. However, the terms "grounder" and "soiler" do not suggest a human being. Hence, the alternate approach seems preferable. As will be discussed below,[21] the best translation for "ADAM" is "human." Hence, the preferred translation of "ADAMAH" is "humus."

Both terms — "human" and "humus" — enter the English language from Latin. While they do not share a common root in Latin or English, the shared initial "hum-" in both words suggests some link, which, for the best sense of our narrative, is desirable. The Latin term, "humus" literally means "ADAMAH," viz., "soil," "land," "earth," "ground," "territory," and/or a "country." In English, "humus" has a more narrow meaning. It is especially rich organic soil. As such, from the perspective of agriculture, it is a positive value term. Furthermore, humus usually is formed out of the decomposition of different kinds of vegetation. Hence, the term, "humus" contributes in several ways to a verbal picture that seems most appropriate to this stage of our narrative. First, the ADAMAH is not just the surface of earth directly facing the sky; it is that surface covered with vegetation. Second, this land surface should be understood to be especially rich soil. As of yet no land has been cultivated. Once it is farmed, that land will begin to deteriorate in its human value. In other words, the ground surface of

---

[21] In connection with Gen 1:26.

our model is paradigmatic soil, i.e., virgin soil, i.e., soil so rich that all of the surface of the dry land can be called "humus." Third, the expression, "creeper of the humus" establishes a closer link between the earth-originated creeper and the two kinds of animals. As the animals are distinguished, not by what they do, but by the way they have value for humans, so the third member of this class is (at least in part) defined relative to its human value, viz., as fresh life that is closely associated with rich farmable land.

וירא אלהים כי־טוב:
VA-YAR ELOHIM KI-TOV
while God perceives that it is excellent.

This is the sixth instance of God judging something to have value (TOV). First there was light,[22] then the seas and the dry land,[23] then the vegetation,[24] then the lighters,[25] then the life that originates from the water,[26] and now the life that originates from the earth.

Genesis 1:26

ויאמר אלהים נעשה אדם בצלמנו כדמותנו
VA-YOMER ELOHIM NA'ASEH ADAM Be-TZALMAINU KADMUTAINU
God says, "Let us make a human in our image (and) in our likeness

This is the eighth time that God orders something through a speech-act (YOMER). God orders a light[27] on day one, a spread[28] on the second day, and lighters[29] on the fourth day all to be-become. Furthermore, he tells the water to congeal to form the division between

---

[22] Gen 1:4, on day one.
[23] Gen 1:10, on the third day.
[24] Gen 1:12, also on the third day.
[25] Gen 1:18, on the fourth day.
[26] Gen 1:21, on the fifth day.
[27] Gen 1:3.
[28] Gen 1:6.
[29] Gen 1:14.

dry land and seas[30] and the earth to sprout a sprout[31] on the third day, the waters to swarm a swarm on the fifth day,[32] and the earth to produce fresh life on the sixth day.[33] Now he verbally orders something quite different.

NA'ASEH is a first person, plural imperfect form of the simple active conjugation of the verb whose root is ayin (ע), shin (ש), he (ה). As an imperfect, the verb expresses a dynamic function that has no limit, i.e., its limit is infinity. The verb already has appeared in our narrative three times. God makes the spread on the second day,[34] the sub-categories of lighters on the fourth day,[35] and the sub-categories of earth-originating fresh life on the sixth day.[36] However, in each of these cases the verb is a third person singular, rather than a first person plural, form of the same conjugation. In other words, in every other case, the maker has been God alone, even when we know that the verb expresses God telling something else to do something, viz., the earth to sprout vegetation and to produce a living thing. Here, the plural number suggests that the action is performed by God together with something else. However, in every other case involving a joint action, God's partner has been named, viz., the water in separating dry land and seas, as well as in swarming water-originating life, and the earth in producing vegetation, as well as making lighters and earth-originating life. Again, here the number of the verb suggests a divine partner, but no partner is named.

These textual anomalies have led different rabbinic commentators to suggest a number of different answers to the question, who are the "us" in "let us make"? By far the most common answer is the angels. Most modern critical commentators agree with this view, as do several sages of the midrash,[37] Saadia,[38] Rashi, Ibn Ezra and Sforno. While this

---

[30] Gen 1:9.
[31] Gen 1:11.
[32] Gen 1:20.
[33] Gen 1:24.
[34] Gen 1:7.
[35] Gen 1:16.
[36] Gen 1:25.
[37] Notably Rabbi Chanina, Rabbi Huna, Rabbi Aibu, Rabbi Jonathan, and Rabbi Samuel Ben Nachman.

answer is certainly coherent with the entire corpus of the Hebrew Scriptures, I do not think that it fits our narrative, primarily because there is nothing in our text to suggest that angels are part of the ontology of this model for the origin of the universe.[39]

Of the candidates suggested by the rabbinic commentators for God's partner in making an ADAM, the least likely are the previous five days of creation[40] and the souls of the righteous.[41] In contrast, the most likely interpretations are the following three: First, there is no partner. God is simply invoking what is called the "royal we."[42] Second, God's partners are the earth and the sky.[43] As God's productions on the fifth day involve the space of the waters with the sky, so God's productions on the sixth day (viz., animals, creepers and an ADAM) involve the earth with the sky. Third, God's partner is God's wind.[44] The textual basis for this judgment is clear. The above textual analysis would suggest that God's partner differs qualitatively from anything else mentioned as a co-producer. It should be something mentioned within the narrative that, in one sense, is distinct from God (to account for the use of the plural), but, in another sense, is identical with him (to account for the use of the first person and the fact that only God is named as an actor).

All three views seem plausible readings of our text. However, my own judgment comes close to the second "likely" interpretation given above. I think that God is speaking to the earth. In general, the work of

---

[38] Viz., Saadia Ben Joseph Al-Fayyumi (@855-@955 CE).
[39] Unless we consider the "lighters" to be angels. In fact this is the interpretation of Saadia, Ibn Ezra, and Sforno, for whom the constellations are governed by separate intellects, and these celestial intellects are called "angels" in the Hebrew Scriptures.
[40] *Genesis Rabbah* attributes this view to Rabbi Samuel Ben Nachman and Rabbi Chama Ben Rabbi Chanina.
[41] *Genesis Rabbah* attributes this view to Rabbi Levi and Rabbi Joshua of Siknin.
[42] *Genesis Rabbah* attributes this view to Rabbi Hila, Rabbi Ammi and Rabbi Jassi.
[43] *Genesis Rabbah* attributes this view to Rabbi Joshua Ben Levi. It is also the view of Nachmanides.
[44] *Genesis Rabbah* attributes this view to Rabbi Simlai.

the sixth day consists of God ordering the earth to generate fresh life. First he generates the animals and creepers, and here he generates the ADAM. There is no need to mention the earth again, given the context of the previous two verses. In other words, given that this verse stipulates that God once again is producing something by ordering a specific region of space to act in a certain way, the most obvious candidate for a direct originator of this particular form of life is the earth.[45]

The model for the partnership between God and the earth is political. As a king may order his scholars (for example) to write a translation of the Bible and thereby share with them the authorship of the product (e.g., the so-called "King James" English translation), so God orders his minister, the earth, to produce a living occupant. What God joins the earth in making is <u>ADAM</u>. The term is a singular, masculine noun. It is not a proper name. Rather, like the sprout (DESHE) of the third day, the swarm (SHERETZ) of the fifth day, and the fresh life (NEFESH CHAYAH) of the sixth day, it is a prototype, whose ontological place within the picture of our textual model functions to explain the infinite power of the earth that enables its occupants to reproduce without beginning or end. In other words, from the perspective of reproduction, there is no first nor last human being. ADAM is not a first person; rather, he is an object situated in a model that accounts for endless human procreation. This particular earth-originating fresh life is distinct from others in two ways. First, God is specified as a partner in his origin. Second, ADAM originates in ADAMAH, i.e., earth covered with vegetation that decays into the most excellent kind of soil.[46] In other words, this life form is special in that it originates in "humus," and, hence, is called a "human."

---

[45] I see nothing in the text to suggest that the sky also is an originator, particularly since, on the fifth day, fliers (the most likely candidates to originate from the spread of the sky) clearly are said to originate from the waters.

[46] When gardeners show off "the work of their hands" to non-gardeners, they show the crops. However, when they show off to fellow gardeners, they show their compost heap. It is the quality of the collected decayed matter that is their real creation. It alone is their contribution to the quality of the produce. Every other variable — e.g.,

Day 6

The particular richness[47] of his origin enables our narrative to claim that the human is something that is in both the "TZELEM" and the "KADMUT" of God and the earth. TZELEM is a masculine noun whose root is tsadik (צ), lamed (ל), mem (ם). It occurs fifteen times in the Hebrew Scriptures.[48] The verbs formed from this root — TZILEM (to photograph) and TZULAM/HITZTALEM (to be photographed) — are creations of modern Hebrew from the biblical noun. In this and the next verse of our narrative,[49] the noun expresses some kind of similarity between the human and God. Of particular interest is the use of the noun in its two appearances in the Psalms. Psalm 73:20 mentions the TZELEM of human beings as something that God will despise, and Psalm 39:7 says that a man (ISH) walks as a TZELEM, where the context makes it clear that this is something of no value (HEVEL). Similarly, in every other appearance, TZELEM expresses something negative, viz., the figures that idolators craft as part of their ritual. In other words, a TZELEM is a figure or image that seems to be uniquely associated with the work of sacred artists, viz., those who create physical objects to function in communal worship. In every case, to call something a "image" seems to have a negative connotation. Hence, while the human is in God's "image," the sense is that he is MERELY an image.

I suspect that the negative sense of the noun has to do with an implicit ontology in our narrative that admits of degrees of reality. In general, something that is a figure of something else is less real than its original. Hence, while a human is something rich by comparison with every other occupant that space generates, he remains, nonetheless, a mere "figure," i.e., something less perfect/excellent, and consequently, less real, than his divine original.[50] In this ontology, the notions of real,

---

the amount of sun and rain — is out of their control. These variables are, in religious language, the work of God.

[47] The pun is intentional.

[48] In Gen 1:26, 27; 5:3; 9:6; Nu 33:52; 1 Sam 6:5, 11; 2 Kgs 11:18; Ez. 7:20; 16:17; 23:14; Amos 5:26; Ps. 39:7; 73:20; 2 Chron 23:17.

[49] Also, in Gen 9:6.

[50] In Plato's *Timaeus*, the occupants of space (viz., the receptacle) are mere reflections (or, figures) that space reflects. In Plato's text the picture is of mirror images, where the mirror that reflects its shapes also creates them. Plato's model of the relationship between space and

perfect, and complete entail each other. God is most real. Next are the divisions of space. Next is the human, and finally are the other varieties of fresh life.[51]

DMUT is a feminine noun formed from a verb whose root is daled (ד), mem (מ), he (ה). The noun often means "likeness," "form," "shape," "resemblance," "figure," and/or "character." Both the noun and the verb occur frequently in the Hebrew Scriptures. Ezekiel often uses the noun in conjunction with the term, "MAREH,"[52] which means something that is seen, viz., an appearance and/or a vision. Similarly, in 2 Kgs. 16:10, the term is used interchangeably with "TAVNIT" (form, model, pattern, figure, image, paradigm, and/or structure) as a model for constructing an altar. The verb can have two very different meanings. On one hand, it often means to "be like" and/or "resemble." On the other hand, it can also mean to "cease," "stop," and/or "destroy." Clearly the term "DMUT" in our text is meant to be interchanged with the term "TZELEM," where together they share the variety of meanings of the English term, "figure." However, whereas the term "image" (TZELEM) adds the negative connotation of something of comparatively lesser value, the term "likeness" (DMUT) adds the sense of something perishable. In other words, for all of the exalted status of the human as a prototype within our model that shares common characteristics with his generators, he remains, nonetheless, inferior to them as something perishable.

Both terms — image and likeness — suggest that in some respect the human is, and in another respect is not, like both God and the earth. The analogy to the earth is clear. Like the earth, the human originates in and consists of the stuff of the earth; unlike the earth, the human is a transient occupant of the intransient space of the earth region. In the

---

spatial individuals seems most appropriate to our narrative's description of the best (viz., most perfect/complete/real) of spatial individuals (viz., the human) still being nothing more than a mere figure.
[51] This implicit ontology of entities whose "degree of reality" vary will be developed by the medieval rabbinic philosophers into an explicit cosmology. For that purpose they will draw heavily from both Aristotle's *De Caelo* and Plato's *Timaeus* in commenting extensively on our narrative.
[52] Cf. Ezek 1:10, 26, 28; 8:2; 10:10; and 23:15.

case of God, the analogy is less clear. While there is no difficulty in saying how God and the human differ, the question remains, how are they alike. In my judgment, the answer lies in the next half of this verse.

וירדו בדגת הים ובעוף השמים
Ve-YIRDU BIDGAT HA-YAM U-Ve-'OF HA-SHAMAYIM
to subdue the fish of the sea, the flier of the sky,

ובבהמה ובכל־הארץ ובכל־הרמש הרמשת על־הארץ:
UV-BeHEMAH UV-KOL-HA-ARETZ UV-KOL-HA-REMES HA-ROMESET 'AL-HA-ARETZ
the domestic animal, all (wild life of) the land, and every creeper that creeps upon the land."

YIRDU is a third person, plural form of the imperfect tense in the simple active conjunction of a verb whose root is resh (ר), daled (ד), he (ה). As an imperfect, it expresses a dynamic function. Because the vowel of conjunction (Ve-) does not combine with the verb here under the rule of the Waw Consecutive, there is no finite limit or end to the activity. In other words, there is neither beginning nor end to the human performance of this activity. While the verb occurs frequently in the Hebrew Scriptures, this is its only appearance in this precise form.[53] In general, the verb means to "rule," "subdue," "subjugate," "punish," and/or "chastise." The sense is that of a governor who governs more through fear than through the consent of those subject to the government. Given that, as we shall see below, the primary use that this governor (the human) will make of his subjects (the fresh life) is as food,[54] the verb's sense of tyrannical rule is appropriate.[55] At the same

---

[53] It occurs twice (in Ps 49:15 and Neh 9:28) as a third person, plural form of the imperfect tense in the simple active conjunction with the vowel of conjunction functioning as a Waw Consecutive (VA-). It also occurs once in this form without a consonant (in Jer 5:31).

[54] I.e., after the expulsion from the Garden of Eden. In our narrative only vegetation is designated as food. However, Abel sacrifices domestic animals with God's approval (Gen 4:4), and the descendants of Noah are given every other living thing as food (Gen 9:2-3).

time, while this government is "tyranny" from the perspective of the other forms of life on the planet, from the perspective of the government of the universe, it is (as we shall see below) judged to have positive value. Hence, "subdue" is, in this context, the preferred English translation, since it expresses the political connotation of the verb, "to rule," adds to its descriptive force the negative sense of "to subjugate" with reference to those governed, without implying that this negative quality of the rulership is, in general, undesirable. In other words, our narrative recognizes that the rule of humans does not serve the best interests of their living subjects, but, at the same time, it does not judge this state to be wrong.

The subjects of human government are life forms that reside in the sea, in the sky, and on the earth. In Genesis 1:20, 21, 24 and 25 the fresh life was subdivided by its origin. The flier and the swarm (which includes the large sea-serpents, the swarming creeper, and the winged flier) originate in the water, while the domestic animal, the land creeper, and the wild animal originate in the earth. Here the living occupants of space are classified by the space they occupy. The fish (<u>DAGAH</u>) resides in the sea. This feminine singular noun includes the previously mentioned large sea-serpents and the swarming creeper. The flier resides in the sky. Finally, the domestic animal, the land creeper, and every wild animal resides on the land. In other words, every form of fresh life generated on the fifth and the sixth days is directly subject to human rule, under the ultimate authority of God. This state of affairs constitutes a description of the sense in which the human is created in the image and likeness of God. The sense is political.[56]

---

[55] Similarly, in Jer 5:31 the sense of the way that the priests rule (YIRDU) Israel is negative, viz., their government is a tyrannical one in that it does not serve the well being of the nation.

[56] According to Rashi, "TZALMAINU" means unqualified power to rule over sea-originated fresh life, and "KADMUTAINU" means that humans have knowledge and understanding, in virtue of which (i.e., to the extent it is developed) they merit (ZAKHAH) to govern land-originated fresh life. In other words, the similarity is that both God and the human are governors. Similarly, according to Ibn Ezra, God and the human share an ability to possess and use theoretical wisdom in order to govern themselves and others. In contrast, Sforno states that God and

That the human will subdue the fresh life is not a commandment; rather, it is a description of what the human will do, viz., he will govern all the fresh life that originate in the water and the earth. This second half of verse 26, following directly upon the first half, makes one an interpretation of the other. As God governs the universe as a whole, and the regions of space under his direction govern their occupants, so the human, under the joint direction of God's will and the nature he receives from the earth, will govern the other occupants of his spatial sphere. His domain includes the occupants of the dry land, the seas, and the sky.

<u>Genesis 1:27</u>

ויברא אלהים את־האדם בצלמו
VA-YIVRA ELOHIM ET-HA-ADAM Be-TZALMO
God gods the human in his image;

This is the second time[57] in our narrative that God gods something. On the fifth day he orders the water to swarm a swarm of fresh life,[58] which is immediately described as God godding the three varieties of this living thing.[59] God's "godding" consists of God ordering direct action by the water. Similarly, on the sixth day, he

---

the human are similar in having choice and in having the potential to become an immortal intellect. The most original answer is Rosenzweig's. He claims that God and man are similar in having personality ("Persönlichkeit," which is one sense of the term, DMUT), which for him is an ontological category that transcends both class and individual member of a class. In other words, according to Rosenzweig what God and the human share in common is that both are defined by their singularity. This second clause of our verse supports the interpretations of Rashi and Ibn Ezra.

[57] Excluding the opening verse, which, as we have seen, stands outside of the narrative, in the same way that the title of a story is not itself part of the story.
[58] Gen 1:20.
[59] Viz., great sea serpents, every creeping swarm, and every winged flier. Gen 1:21.

orders the earth to produce fresh life,[60] which is immediately followed by God making its three varieties.[61] God's "making" on the sixth day and "godding" on the fifth day are the same kinds of acts. Consider John Wilkes Booth pulling the trigger of a gun, the trigger firing a bullet, and the bullet killing Abraham Lincoln. These three, verbally distinct acts, are in reality a single event, viz., Booth killing Lincoln with a gun. In precisely the same way, God godding/making fresh life with the space of water/earth is a single event. Similarly, God orders the earth to make a human,[62] which is immediately described as God godding the two varieties of this living thing. The varieties are two genders — male and female. The earth/God-generated human is neither a hermaphrodite, nor androgynous, nor two different human beings. He is a model. While the noun, ADAM, is a masculine singular,[63] he has no gender whatsoever. Rather, he, like all of the other generated occupants of space, is a prototype for both genders.

בצלם אלהים ברא אתו זכר ונקבה ברא אתם:
Be-TZELEM ELOHIM BARA OTO ZAKHAR U-NeKEVAH BARA OTAM
he gods (the human) in the image of God; he gods (their kinds as) male and female.

The verb, "to god," is repeated three times in this verse. This is the third way that the origin of the human differs from that of any other occupant of space. (1) God uses the first person plural in his speech-act to make the human,[64] and, in so doing, he identifies himself as a partner with space in the production. (2) The human is the only occupant of space that is explicitly said to be made in the figure of God,[65] i.e., to have something in common with him, viz., the function of intentional, political rule. (3) The narrative now states three times that God gods the human in his image.

---

[60] Gen 1:24-26.
[61] Viz., domestic-animal, wild-animal, and humus-creeper. Gen 1:25.
[62] Gen 1:26.
[63] And hence, ADAM should be referred to as "he."
[64] Gen 1:26.
[65] I.e., in his "image" and "likeness," in Gen 1:26.

Day 6

We have already noted that this verse is related to the preceding verse as Genesis 1:25 is to Genesis 1:24 and Genesis 1:21 is to Genesis 1:20. Our text first quotes God speaking to a region of space to originate an occupant, and then describes the event in a third person narrative form, where God alone is the actor. In each of these cases the object-to-be-originated in the quoted speech act is a single paradigm that is differentiated into sub-species in the consequent description. However, here, in the case of the human, the description is repeated three times in the following pattern:

Action	Actor	Product	Modification
VA-YIVRA	ELOHIM	ET-HA-ADAM	Be-TZALMO
gods	God	the human	in his image
BARA	—	OTO	Be-TZELEM ELOHIM
gods	(God)	him	in the image of God
BARA	—	OTAM	ZAKHAR U-NeKEVAH
gods	(God)	them	male and female

In all three instances, God gods the human. The three sentences differ only in the construction of the verbs and in the modifications of the product. In all three sentences the verb is "to god" in the third person singular of the simple active conjugation. However, in the first sentence, "gods" is an imperfect tense joined to the consonant of conjunction under the force of the Waw Consecutive, whereas in the next two sentences "gods" is in the perfect tense. The first construction expresses that the production of the human is a dynamic function directed at a stable state limit. The second construction expresses that this production is a stable state. The combination of the two constructions expresses something unique about the generation of the human. In the case of the other fresh life, only the first construction is used,[66] which indicates that their production also is a dynamic, asymptotic function. However, unlike the human, there is considerable distance between their original dynamic state and their final stable end. In contrast, in the case of the human, there is little difference between

---

[66] In Gen 1:21, 25.

the origin and the end. This grammatical analysis accounts for another respect in which the human is uniquely like God. Not only is he an entity with the political capacity to govern; he also has, in his origin, a moral level of excellence that is not shared by his fellow residents of the space of the universe.

Concerning the differences in modifications, the first sentence says that the human is in "his" image, and the second sentence explains that the "his" means God's. In other words, the modifications deal with the human being as a figure of God. In this context, the third modification expresses that to be in God's image applies to both genders of humans. Two matters of interest follow from this analysis. First, since the main terms in each sentence express a dynamic function, directed towards a stable-state end, the modifications express what that end is, viz., to become the figure of God. In other words, the end and/or value of every human, irrespective of gender, is to be-come like God. In other words, the moral principle of the imitation-of-God is the standard by which human life is to be judged of value. Second, this standard entails no distinction, either in origin or end, between males and females.[67]

---

[67] In at least this one respect, the moral ontology of our Genesis narrative differs significantly from its counterpart in Plato's *Timaeus*. Plato also presents a picture of prototypes of individual living things hierarchically ordered according to moral principles, where the relative excellence of different species is judged by the degree to which they approximate the divine originator of the universe. Furthermore, Plato also makes the human the most perfect of physical, living things. However, Plato specifically notes that this most excellent of creatures is masculine. The female human is superior to all other animals, but inferior to the male human. In terms of each narrative's moral view of gender, for Plato women achieve their perfection only through men. Hence, in order to overcome their mortality (i.e., to escape from the process of reincarnation), they must first become men. For the author of our narrative, the origin of the human contains no comparable gender subservience. The female will become subject to the authority of the male (viz., in Gen 3:16). However, this lesser political status has nothing to do with the "nature" of the female human in her origin, and, as such, has nothing to do with our narrative. In other words, the Hebrew Scriptures present the subjugation of women to men as a transitory,

Genesis 1:28

ויברך אתם אלהים ויאמר להם אלהים
VA-YIVAREKH OTAM ELOHIM VA-YOMER LAHEM ELOHIM
God blesses them and God says to them,

פרו ורבו ומלאו את־הארץ וכבשה
PeRU U-RVU U-MIL-U ET-HA-ARETZ Ve-KIVSUHA
"Be fruitful, increase, fill the land, and conquer it;

This is the second time that God blesses a life form with a commandment.[68] On the fifth day he gods/blesses/commands the life that originates from the waters. Now he does the same, in almost the same form. In both cases the verb, <u>YIVAREKH</u>, is a third person, singular form in the imperfect tense of the intensive active conjugation, joined to the consonant of conjunction. The blessing is followed by God saying something, and the something said is a set of imperatives. Furthermore, the first three commands are the same, viz., masculine, plural imperatives that mean "be fruitful," "increase," and "fill" something.

The difference between these two verses is the following: The grammatical form of God's speech-act on the fifth day is an adverb ("LAIMOR"); on the sixth day, the verb has the same form as the blessing (<u>VA-YOMER</u>). Furthermore, on the fifth day, the "something" to be filled is the water in the seas; on the sixth day it is the land. Finally, on the fifth day, the assertion of the three imperatives is followed by a descriptive statement that singles out one of the kinds of entities blessed, viz., the text states that the flier will increase on the land rather than in the seas. In contrast, on the sixth day there is a fourth imperative, viz., what is commanded to be fruitful/increase/fill-the-land is also commanded, "KIVSHUHA."

On the fifth day God speaks to and commands the waters to do something that blesses its occupants. However, it is less obvious who

---

temporal fact of history, much as it presents the subjugation of Israel to other nations. Neither historical occurrence is an inherent feature of the divine structure/order of the universe.

[68] Gen 1:22.

are the objects blessed, spoken to, and commanded on the sixth day. There are four possible candidates for the objects of all three divine acts: The earth, the earth-originating fresh life, the human, and/or male-and-female humans. Whatever the objects are in every case, the gender and number of both the pronouns (OTAM and LAHEM) and the imperatives (PeRU, RVU, MIL-U, and KIVSHU) is masculine plural. The parallel between this verse and Genesis 1:22 would suggest that what is blessed are all of the earth-originating fresh life, including both genders of human, what is commanded is the earth, and the fourth commandment singles out one of the kinds of entities blessed for special mention, viz., the two genders of human. In other words, God blesses every life form that originates from the earth (just as he blesses every life form that originates from the water) by commanding its spatial originator to empower its products to reproduce. Then, a member of the general class of blessed objects is singled out for special mention — the flier in the case of water-originating life, and the human in the case of earth-originating life. On the fifth day, the special mention is a descriptive statement about the flier; on the sixth day, the special mention of the human is an imperative. The difference is that our narrative pictures the human (but not the flier) as something that has the power to govern, and, as such, can be commanded to do something, rather than merely described as be-coming something.

What the two genders of the human are commanded to do is KIVSHUHA. The suffix "HA" is a third person, singular, feminine pronoun. Clearly its referent is the land surface of the earth. "KIVSHU" is a plural imperative in the simple active conjugation of a verb whose root is kaph (כ), bet (ב), shin (ש). This is its only appearance in this form in the Hebrew Scriptures. However, the verb occurs in different forms seven times in this conjugation,[69] five times in the simple passive,[70] and three times in the intensive active.[71] It is the verb that Ahashuerus uses when he accuses Haman of raping Esther.[72] It is most commonly used to describe what a victorious nation does to a

---

[69] Jer 34:11,16; Micah 7:19; Zech 9:15; Esth 7:8; Neh 5:5; 2 Chron 28:10.
[70] Nu 32:22, 29; Josh 18:1; Neh 5:5; 1 Chron 22:18.
[71] 2 Sam 8:11; Jer 34:11.
[72] Esth 7:8.

defeated nation,⁷³ and, in this context, it is associated with making people slaves.⁷⁴ In this spirit, Zechariah⁷⁵ interchanges "KAVSHU" with "AKHLU," which means to "eat" and/or "consume." In other words, "KIVSHU" states what "YIRDU" expressed in Genesis 1:26, only here the sense of negative value and tyranny is even stronger. There God orders the earth to join him in making a human who will "subdue" all forms of life. Here God commands this life form to conquer them, where "to conquer" has all the connotations of conquest, consumption, and even rape.

וּרְדוּ בִדְגַת הַיָּם וּבְעוֹף הַשָּׁמַיִם וּבְכָל־חַיָּה הָרֹמֶשֶׂת עַל־הָאָרֶץ:
U-RDU VIDGAT HA-YAM U-Ve-'OF HA-SHAMAYIM
UV-KOL-CHAYAH HA-ROMESET 'AL-HA-ARETZ
subdue the fish of the sea, the flier of the sky, and all life that creeps upon the land."

The last clause of this verse spells out what it means for the two genders of the human to conquer the land, exhibits the connection between this verse and Genesis 1:26, and reflects the parallelism between the descriptions of the work of the fifth⁷⁶ and the sixth days. On the fifth day, God ordering the water to swarm life is followed by God godding that life, and blessing it through a commandment to reproduce. On the sixth day, God ordering the earth to join him in making the human to subdue all other forms of life is followed by God godding the human, and blessing him through a commandment to conquer all other living things.

---

⁷³ Cf. Nu. 32: 22,29; Josh 18:1; 2 Sam 8:11.
⁷⁴ Cf. Jer 34:11 and Neh 5:5.
⁷⁵ Zech 9:15.
⁷⁶ Gen 1:20-22.

Genesis 1:29

ויאמר אלהים הנה נתתי לכם
VA-YOMER ELOHIM HINEH NATATI LAKHEM
God says, "I appoint for you

את־כל־עשב זרע זרע אשר על־פני־כל־הארץ
ET-KOL-'ESEV ZORE'A ZERA' ASHER 'AL-PeNAI-KOL-HA-ARETZ
every plant that seeds seed which is over all the land,

ואת־כל־העץ אשר־בו פרי־עץ זרע זרע
Ve-ET-KOL-HA-'ETZ ASHER-BO PeRI-'ETZ ZORE'A ZERA'
and every tree that contains tree-fruit that seeds seed;

לכם יהיה לאכלה:
LAKHEM YIHYEH Le-AKHLAH
(each of them) will be food for you.

This is the eleventh,[77] and final, time that God speaks in our narrative. On the days one, two, and four, his speech produces a material (viz., light, spread, and lighters), but it is not directed to anyone or anything. He tells water to congeal and the earth to sprout on day three; water to swarm on day five; earth to produce fresh life and to join him in making the human on day six. Finally, he speaks blessings to the living products of days five and six. His speech has produced a universe that consists primarily of (a) regions of space that are empowered to produce spatial occupants, and (b) spatial occupants that are prototypes of fresh life that possess a temporally limitless capacity to reproduce. What he says now is a political decree.

NATATI is a first person singular form of the perfect tense of the simple active conjugation of the verb whose root is nun (נ), tet (ת), nun (נ). This is the second appearance[78] of this verb in our narrative. On the fourth day, God places the lighters in the spread of the sky to govern day and night by keeping light and dark separate. The sense of "placing" is also political; it means "appointing," i.e., placing one subject in authority over other subjects. There, those placed in authority are the lighters, and those subject to their authority are day and night. Here, those placed in authority (viz., the "for you" [LAKHEM], where the

---

[77] In Gen 1:3, 6, 9, 11, 14, 20, 22, 24, 26, 28.
[78] In Gen 1:17.

pronoun is a second person plural) are the two genders of the human, and those subject to their authority are the different varieties of vegetation.

The verb for governing associated with the political appointment on the fourth day is MASHAL.[79] The sense of this verb is purely descriptive. In itself it says nothing about the excellence or moral quality of the administration. In contrast, the verbs for governing associated with the appointment on day six are RADAH[80] and KAVASH.[81] Both terms suggest that this form of government, whatever its other values, is not intended for the welfare of its subjects. The last word of the sentence makes this negative value clear. Humans have political authority over vegetation in order to eat it.

There is another significant respect in which these two uses of the same verb differ. In verse 17, the tense is an imperfect in the Waw Consecutive, which means that the function ordained for the lighters is the stable end of a dynamic process. In other words, there is no separation between the origin of the act and its ideal end. Here, in verse 29, the use of the perfect indicates a stable state without any dynamic. The action ordained is non-moral. It is an activity that has no end. Whereas the order given to the lighters has to do with preserving something (viz., day and night), the order given to humans has to do with destroying something (viz., vegetation). Because of what the lighters do, dark and light continue to be day and night. The implication is, if not for their action, dark and light would disappear into the original dark that pervaded the entire universe. In contrast, humans are ordained to eat fellow occupants of space. The humans eating has the opposite effect of the lighters enlightening. The enlightening preserves day and night as day and night. In contrast, the eating destroys the separation between what eats and what is eaten. The food ceases to have its own identity; instead, it becomes an indistinguishable part the body of the eater.

---

[79] In Gen 1:16 and 18.
[80] In Gen 1:26.
[81] In Gen 1:28.

Genesis 1:30

ולכל-חית הארץ ולכל-עוף השמים
U-Le-KOL-CHAYAT HA-ARETZ U-Le-KOL-'OF HA-SHAMAYIM
For every land-life of the (planet) earth, for every flier of the sky,

ולכל רומש על-הארץ אשר-בו נפש חיה
U-Le-KOL ROMES 'AL-HA-ARETZ ASHER-BO NEFESH CHAYAH
and for every creeper upon the land in which there is fresh life,

את-כל-ירק עשב לאכלה
ET-KOL-YEREK 'ESEV Le-AKHLAH
will every green plant be food,"

The humans are given authority over all vegetation in order to eat it. The statement is political. In contrast, the statement that the other life forms of the planet earth can eat some vegetation (viz., the "green" [YEREK] variety) is merely descriptive. Like the plants, the animals/birds/insects are subjects who have no share in God's political administration of the universe. Here, we are told that they are eaters. Later, we will discover that they also, like every green plant, are food.[82]

In summary, our narrative presents two human perspectives on all other living things. First, humans bear a divinely ordained responsibility to govern them. Second, from the perspective of this natural polity, all they are is food.[83]

---

[82] In Gen 9:3. The setting is after the flood.

[83] The primary interest throughout the Pentateuch with these life forms is (a) which ones can you sacrifice, and (b) which ones can you eat. Subsequent rabbinic Judaism will tend to divide them into the primary categories of "TEREFAH" (what you cannot eat) and "KASHER" (what you can eat), where the KASHER variety is subdivided into the MILKHIC (what you cannot eat with the FLEISCHIC), the FLEISHIC (what you cannot eat with the MILKHIC), and the PAREVE (what you can eat with anything KASHER).

Day 6

וַיְהִי־כֵן:
VA-YeHIY-KHEN
and it becomes so.

This is the sixth and final time that our narrative declares something to be true. We are told that the spread separates waters,[84] and seas and dry land;[85] the earth produces vegetation;[86] the lighters enlighten the earth;[87] water and earth produce life;[88] and now, life eats life. Plants exist to be eaten by insects, birds, animals, and humans. This truth judgment about food concludes our narrative's description of the model of our present universe. What remains is the final judgment about the moral value of the model in its entirely[89] and the introduction of the dimension of time,[90] so that the author of Genesis can move beyond the physical sciences[91] to the human sciences.[92]

Genesis 1:31

וַיַּרְא אֱלֹהִים אֶת־כָּל־אֲשֶׁר עָשָׂה וְהִנֵּה־טוֹב מְאֹד
VA-YAR ELOHIM ET-KOL-ASHER 'ASAH Ve-HINEH-TOV MeOD
God perceives (that) all he makes is very excellent.

This is the seventh time[93] that God perceives something. In every case the perception is a judgment that the object perceived has virtue. The objects judged are light, the seas and dry land, vegetation, lighters, and the living things that occupy every kind of space. Each object is defined by a function, where that action is understood in terms of an asymptote. In other words, objects are not primarily conceived of as

---

[84] Gen 1:7.
[85] Gen 1:9.
[86] Gen 1:11.
[87] Gen 1:15.
[88] Gen 1:24.
[89] Gen 1:31.
[90] Gen 2:1-3.
[91] Physics, astronomy, biology, zoology, agronomy, etc.
[92] History, political science, sociology, etc.
[93] Cf. Gen 1:4, 10, 12, 18, 21 and 25.

things. Rather, they are described dynamically as directed action, whose limit or end defines the object. Hence, our narrative perceiving an object to be excellent is, in effect, a judgment that the events of the universe are to be understood as goal directed actions. In other words, whereas actions are real, objects are ideal, and it is the ideal that defines the real.

What God perceives now is everything that he made. "Everything" means primarily the differentiation of space into a central earth core, containing a spread that separates the core from the encircling waters, all subject to an alternating spatial characterization of being filled with elementary light and dark. Furthermore, "everything" means the powers of this space to produce an endless number of residents, whose reproduction is unlimited with respect to time. These occupants are life forms, whose origin is either in water or earth. The space that they occupy during their brief appearance as individual members of their species is the land (composed of elementary earth), the sea (composed of elementary water) or the sky (composed of elementary spread). These living things are defined primarily by what they most characteristically do. Some of them sprout, others enlighten, and others fly, swarm, creep, walk, and/or eat in and/or on their space. Together, all of them — the space and its residents — constitute a polity. The supreme ruler is God, who delegates his authority to ministers. The lighters govern the sky in order to preserve the separation between light and dark. Conversely, the humans govern the earth in order to turn its residents into food.

All of this God judges to be "very (MeOD) excellent." While all of the parts are simply judged "excellent," the whole is "very excellent," which means, whatever the virtues of the parts, their value ultimately resides in the role they play in perfecting the whole. The universe in its entirely is to be understood not as a "thing," but, like its parts, as a unified activity, directed towards a limit or end.[94]

---

[94] The rabbis will describe that end in messianic terms, i.e., the value of this present world of time and space lies not in "this world," but in another world, a "world to come," that is the end of this world. The term, "end" is to be understood in all of its ambiguity. It is an end to the line of time; it is a limit to all processes within the universe; it is the moral standard by which all of those processes are to be judged.

Day 6

ויהי־ערב ויהי בקר יום הששי:
VA-YeHIY-'EREV VA-YeHIY VOKER YOM HA-SHISHI
The sixth day there is evening and morning.

Day one is unique because of the use of a cardinal number ("ECHAD"). Every other day is identified by an ordinal number. The difference suggests something unique about this day, viz., that the division of creation into multiple acts does not reflect the reality of the event; in fact, God godding the universe is a single, atemporal action. Similarly, there is something special about the last two days of our model. The sixth and the seventh days differ from days two through five, because of the use of the definite article (HA-) with the the ordinal number. Whereas our text states "a" second, third, fourth, and fifth day; here we find "the" sixth (HA-SHISHI) and "the" seventh day. As we shall see, what is special about the seventh day is that it introduces the dimension of time into what otherwise is a purely spatial model. The sixth day differs from the days that precede it in a number of respects.

On days one and two, God's action is described by four verbs, that produce a single elementary stuff, that makes a single division in space. On day one, God says, perceives, separates, and names in order to produce a light that divides day and night. On day two, God speaks, makes, separates, and names in order to produce a spread that divides the waters with the space of the sky. On day three, God is the subject of five verbs in order to perform two actions. He concludes the differentiation of space by saying, naming, and perceiving the water in order to divide the seas and the earth; and he begins the production of living things by ordering and perceiving the earth in order to originate vegetation. God's action on the fourth day is expressed through four verbs (saying, making, placing, and perceiving) that produces the lighters that reside in the sky. On day five, God's production of what the waters originate involves five verbs, viz., saying, godding, perceiving, blessing, and saying. Finally, on the sixth day, God produces the residents of the earth. However, this day stands out in at least two respects. First, he is the subject of twelve verbs. He says (1:24), makes and perceives (1:25), says again (1:26), gods three times (1:27), blesses and says (1:28), says and appoints (1:29), and, finally, perceives (1:31). Second, he ordains one thing (the human) to eat other things. Whereas every other action is directed at producing and preserving separations, at least this one action is intended to relate what otherwise is separate to a point that, at the level of the individual event, the two become one (viz., the eater and the food become the eater). In the end, created order through spatial/physical separation gives way to the activity of living, whose end is physical/political unity.

Day 7

Genesis 2:1

ויכלו השמים והארץ וכל-צבאם:
VA-YeKHULU HA-SHAMAYIM Ve-HA-ARETZ Ve-KOL-TZeVA-AM
The sky, the earth and all their objects are finished.

YeKHULU is a third person plural form in the imperfect tense in the intensive passive conjugation, joined to the consonant of conjunction, of a verb whose root is kaph (כ), lamed (ל), he (ה). This is the first of three verbs that occur for the first time in our narrative. The other two are "YISHBOT"[1] and "YeKADESH".[2] This fact alone indicates that there is something special about the seventh day that distinguishes it from the previous six days. Another significant sign is that this is the only day on which "YOMER" does not appear. In general, God produces the universe primarily through speech-acts. In this respect our story is complete; whatever God has to say has been said. As we shall see, this is precisely what "YeKHULU" means.

The verb is passive; its subjects are the earth, the sky, and their "TZeVA." "Earth" and "sky" name the primary division of space stipulated at the beginning of our narrative in Genesis 1:1. It includes the two regions of water. Presumably the upper water belongs to the sky, and the lower water belongs to the earth. TZeVA-AM is a masculine

---

[1] Gen 2:2.
[2] Gen 2:3.

noun with a third person, plural, masculine suffix, where the noun is formed from a verb, whose root is tzadik (צ), bet (ב), aleph (א). The verb means to (1) "assemble," "gather together," (2) "wage war," and/or (3) "perform service" (with specific reference to the Temple cult). In this case the primary meaning of the noun, "TZeVA," is derived from the first sense of the verb. The suffix, "-AM," is a third person plural possessive pronoun that refers to the space of the universe (viz., the earth and the sky), and the noun refers collectively to its occupants. In other words, the term "TZeVA-AM" refers collectively to the objects that occupy, and are generated by, this space — viz., the lighters of the sky, the swarms of the water, and the fresh life of the earth. In other words, the subject of the verb is every place and every object produced on days one through six.

At the same time the second and third noted senses of the verbal root of the noun cannot be ignored. The term preserves the connotation of forces mustered in both military and priestly service. The purpose of living things is understood in terms of its relation to the Temple cult. Furthermore, as the verbs chosen to express the human's obligation to govern them exhibit, the political model for the relationship between the universe's subjects and its various levels of rulers is one of conquest. The ruler does not exist for the sake of his subjects; on the contrary, they exist to serve (both literally and figuratively) him.

This is the only instance of this conjugation (viz., intensive passive) of any verb in our narrative. Furthermore, this particular verb appears nowhere else in the Hebrew Scriptures in this precise form. However, the verb occurs often in the simple active conjugation, as it does in the next verse where God is the subject. In other words, what God does in the next verse is what happens to the entire universe in this verse.

Genesis 2:2

ויכל אלהים ביום השביעי מלאכתו אשר עשה
VA-YeKHAL ELOHIM BA-YOM HA-SHeVI'I MeLAKHTO ASHER 'ASAH
On the seventh day God finishes his task which he makes,

YeKHAL is a third person singular form in the imperfect tense in the simple active conjugation, joined to the consonant of conjunction, of a verb whose root is kaph (כ), lamed (ל), he (ה). In this construction the verb expresses a dynamic action that has an asymptotic end. It can mean to "finish," "complete," and/or "end." Clearly this is the intended meaning in our narrative. The verb appears five more times in the Pentateuch in this form. In four instances the verb expresses that the subject has finished speaking.[3] The remaining case, Exodus 40:33, most closely parallels our present context. There we are told that Moses finishes the task (MeLAKHAH) that God has assigned to him, viz., to build the tabernacle of the tent of meeting. In other words, God brings the universe — both its space and its occupants — to its completion (in the sense of state, viz., that which is the standard for truth judgment) and its end (in the sense of perfection, viz., that which is the standard for moral judgment).

This root can also mean to "finish" in the sense of to "destroy" and/or to "consume." The feminine noun, KHALAH, derives its meanings of "extinction" and "extermination" from these senses of the verb. In this respect it is interesting to note that day six concludes with a reference to eating. Clearly, divine eating, through the sacrificial system of the priestly cult, occupies a central place in specifying the end or purpose of God godding the universe. In this respect, for God to "finish" creation means that the universe is established for the end of consumption.

The universe is a dynamic something that is defined in terms of both an origin and an end. We have already noted that the origin is negative.[4] Now we see that the end also is negative. As the human both arises from and returns to the humus, so the universe itself both arises from and returns to nothing.

Both the positive and the negative sense of the verb introduces something new into our narrative. The description of days one through six draws a picture of a universe within the dimensions of space. Day seven introduces the dimension of time. As the origin is prior to the world, and, as such, is associated with the past, so the end is posterior to the world, and is associated with the future. The verb conveys the sense of an action that moves from the past to the future, and, as such,

---

[3] God to Abraham in Gen 17:22; Jacob to his sons in Gen 49:33; and Moses to Israel in Ex 34:33 and Dt 32:45.

[4] In Gen 1:2. The initial earth and water are devoid of value (TOHU VAVOHU), and the other givens — depth and dark — are negative entities.

introduces the sense of a universe whose dimensionality includes time. The past and the future are static; only the present is dynamic, and, as dynamic, it is transitory or ephemeral. It is defined by what was and what will be, but, in itself, as the present moment, it is not anything. This sense of the verb is the basis for its form as an adjective, KALEH, which means "transitory" and/or "ephemeral."

What God finishes is his "MeLAKHAH." "MeLAKHAH" is a feminine noun whose masculine counterpart is "MALAKH." The masculine term, often mistranslated as "angel," is used throughout the Hebrew Scriptures to designate a divine messenger, i.e., someone in direct relation to God who performs some service for him. Although the term is not used specifically in our narrative, clearly God's "messengers" are the lighters (that govern day-light and night-dark), the waters (that swarm fresh-life), the earth (that produces fresh-life), and the two genders of the human (that subdue and conquer all of the swarmed and produced fresh-life). What it is that they do for him, in response to his speech-act, is <u>MeLAKHTO</u>, his task, viz., the production of the entire universe.

וישבת ביום השביעי מכל־מלאכתו אשר עשה:
VA-YISHBOT BA-YOM HA-SHeVI'I MI-KOL-MeLAKHTO ASHER 'ASAH
and on the seventh day he rests from all of his task which he makes.

<u>YISHBOT</u> is the second of the three verbs that appear in our narrative for the first time in connection with the seventh day. It is a third person, singular imperfect tense, joined to the consonant of conjunction, in the simple active conjugation of a verb whose root is shin (ש), bet (ב), taf (ת). It usually means to "rest," "cease," "stop," and/or "come to an end." The noun formed from the verb is the Shabbat. The noun indicates the second primary sense of the verb, which is "to observe the regulations of the Sabbath." In terms of its first set of meanings, "YISHBOT" is a synonym for "YeKHAL." As such, verse 1 and both clauses in verse 2 assert the same thing, viz., that the process of generation in space carried out on days one through six is finished on day seven, which introduces, independent of any direct action by God, the dimension of time. However, the second meaning of "YISHBOT" adds connotations that the first verb lacks. To cease and/or become complete and/or achieve an end-limit entails to observe the Sabbath.

This entailment is spelled out in the rest of the Pentateuch. In general, "observance" involves distinct obligations for both space and its occupants. The occupants commanded to observe the Sabbath are the human, or, to be more precise, a single sub-category of human. In history the product of human procreation will be divided into nations, and one of those nations, viz., Israel, will be separated from the rest to serve God in special ways. One of the more notable "ways" is to observe the Sabbath. Similarly, the space commanded to observe the Sabbath is the earth, or, to be more precise, a single sub-category of the earth. Again, in history the land will be divided into national territories, and one of those territories, viz., the land of Israel, will be separated from all others to serve God in special ways, one of which is to observe his Sabbath. Both Sabbaths are defined in terms of time. There is a cessation of work/process on every seventh day, on every seventh year, and on every fiftieth year. The first is the Sabbath day. It begins in the evening and ends in the morning. Its time is measured by the alterations of day-light and night-dark. The second is the Sabbath year (viz., the Sabbatical).[5] The third is the Sabbath of Sabbaticals (viz., the Jubilee).[6] Both the Sabbatical and the Jubilee are measured by the cycle of the motion of the lighters in the sky. These cultic ends/limits/values, whose observance is distinguished by ending/ceasing/resting, constitute the ends/ending that govern the lighters' rule of the sky and the humans' subjugation of the earth and its inhabitants.

As the introduction of light, as distinct from dark, on the first day makes the primordial dark into something,[7] so the introduction of

---

[5] Viz., the year of "SHeMITAH" when the land is left fallow.

[6] Viz., the fiftieth year (i.e., the year following 7x7 [a Sabbath of Sabbaths] years), called the "YOVEL," when all privately owned land reverts to its original owner. It is a system of national land reform in which, to use the schema of Genesis, natural human ambition to expand private ownership also comes to an end/cessation in rest. Among other purposes it demonstrates who the real owner of the land is, viz., God. (Once more, in this respect as well, the world- and life-view of the Hebrew Scriptures affirm that the universe [including the human] exists for the sake of God, and not God for its sake.)

[7] Viz., light, in its opposition to dark, is day; dark, in its opposition to light, is night. Day and night are the something that light and dark become through their

cessation, as distinct from action, on the seventh day makes the divine task on the first six days something, for space without time is not yet anything. The generation of space and its occupants, in opposition to God's rest, is past. The rest of God/space/its occupants, in opposition to his action, is future. Past and future are something that the seven days of God godding the universe become through their separation. The past of the first six days and the future of the seventh define our temporal world, where every lived moment in history is in the present. Together they are only a model that is independent of human and physical history; one defines the other by not being it, and, as such, sets the parameters of our lived universe in space-time.

Genesis 2:3

ויברך אלהים את־יום השביעי ויקדש אתו

VA-YeVAREKH ELOHIM ET-YOM HA-SHeVI'I VA-YeKADESH OTO

God blesses the seventh day and sanctifies it,

The seventh (Sabbath) day is the third thing that God blesses. On the fifth day he blesses the living forms that the waters swarm,[8] and on the sixth day he blesses the two genders of human being.[9] Both are blessed with an unlimited capacity to procreate individual members of their species. In addition, the human is given political dominion over the other living forms that the earth produces. Here God blesses the seventh day when he "YeKADESH" it.

YeKADESH is the third verb that appears in our narrative for the first time in connection with the seventh day. It is a third person, masculine, singular form in the imperfect tense of the intensive active conjugation, joined to the consonant of conjunction, of a verb whose root is kuf (ק), daled (ד), shin (ש). It can mean to "sanctify," "consecrate," "hallow," "declare holy," "purify," and/or "cleanse." Here the actor is God and the direct object is the seventh day. When the actor is human, the verb can have several, different, precise meanings

---

separation from each other. Independently, without separation, they are not anything; one defines the other by not being it.

[8] Gen 1:22.
[9] Gen 1: 28.

that are determined by the direct object. If the actor is a man and the direct object is a woman or the man's daughter, then the verb means, "to betroth." If the direct object is a war (MILCHAMAH), then the verb means "to declare or wage war." Furthermore, if the direct object is God's name, then it means "to become a martyr." The noun and the object formed from the verb all mean "holy." The Temple was called "the holy thing" (KODESH); its sacrifices were also called "holy things" (KADASHIM); the land of Israel in which it was located was called a "holy land" (ERETZ HA-KODESH), and its central sanctuary was called "the most holy of holy things" (KODESH HA-KADASHIM). In every case it is something made special by becoming pure and clean. These last two English modifications express the sense of the verb as an action that makes its object separate. In other words, God's final act in our narrative is once again to make a separation. As space is ordered by regions becoming separate, so time itself is ordered by the-until-now-unified days becoming distinct. The sense in which the seventh day is separate from the others was explained in the preceding verse. The other days are past; the seventh is future. The other days define space; the seventh defines time. The other days express an end-directed process; the seventh expresses the end/limit/goal/value of that process. What the verb "to sanctify" adds to the description in the previous verse is the distinct character of the seventh day as God's possession. When actors sanctify objects, they designate them as something special and separate, that belongs to the actors. A woman betrothed can be married to none other than the man who betroths her. In this sense she belongs to him. Similarly, when God sanctifies something, he betroths it. The holy land, people, and time are set aside from all other lands, peoples, and times as his special possessions. Hence, the process of divine separation that our narrative describes has come to an end, but the end is only a cessation of direct, divine fiat. The process that God initiates by ordaining its end out of its origin will produce in history other separations, the most important of which will be to set aside God's holy land, people, and sanctuary.

כי בו שבת מכל־מלאכתו אשר־ברא אלהים לעשות:
KI VO SHAVAT Me-KOL-MeLAKHTO ASHER-BARA ELOHIM LA'ASOT
because on it he rests from all of his task which God gods by making.

Our commentary began with an unresolved discussion of what "BARA" could mean. This last phrase of the narrative gives us our answer. It is a general term for "making." <u>BARA</u> is one of two things in the Hebrew Scriptures that only God does.[10] It describes a single act that is expressible through multiple speech-acts by which God commands his messengers to perform the task of differentiating space into distinct regions that generate life forms ordered into a political hierarchy whose ultimate *raison d'etre* is to serve God through his intended sacrificial cult. His task of issuing commands is now complete, but the program he ordains is still being carried out. So far the original nothing has produced spatial separations between the regions of sky and earth in which land and seas are distinguished. These regions in turn produce separations between fresh living occupants of this space. Those that swarm from the sea are distinct from those that are produced by the earth. Similarly, the residents of the sky, the seas, and the earth are separate. In the sea, the large sea-serpents, the creepers, and the winged fliers are distinct. Similarly, in the sky, the sun, the moon, and the other celestial objects are distinct. All of these lighters are administrators, whose primary duty is to preserve the separation of day and night, so that different periods of time can be measured, so that the human messengers who will be in charge of the Temple will know what to sacrifice when and how. Similarly, on the earth the creepers, the wild animals and the domestic animals are distinct. All of them are subject to

---

[10] The other verb whose subject always is God has the root samekh (ס), lamed (ל), chet (ח). Cf., Jacob Milgrom's commentary on Numbers in *The JPS Torah Commentary* (Philadelphia/New York, The Jewish Publication Society, 1990) Excursus 32, pp. 395-396. The usual translation of this verb is "to pardon." However, as Milgrom indicates, this term no more has the ordinary sense of pardoning than "BARA" has of creating. Both terms express ways that God acts as God, viz., that God gods. They are not different because of what God does; rather, they differ because of the object that receives God's single act. In the case of "SALACH," the object is the human; in the case of "BARA," the object is the universe.

the government of the human, whose primary duty is to control them. As in the case of the occupants of the seas, the subjects of human domination are obligated to sustain themselves on the provided vegetation, so that they will reproduce endlessly, so that the human will have an unlimited supply of sacrifices to God. What remains to be done is to introduce additional separations within human history. The Semites (viz., the descendents of Abraham) are to separate themselves from Non-semites (through the commandment of circumcision), the Hebrews are to separate themselves from the Semites (through the laws of Moses) by becoming the nation of Israel, and, finally the Levites are to separate themselves from the rest of Israel by directly performing sacrifices for God. In other words, the model of the universe presented in Genesis is, first and foremost, an interpretation of the meaning of the daily activity of the priests, who undoubtedly understood their divine function as the single most important activity in the universe.

Conclusion

The interest in a philosophical analysis of any text will always be more than merely to unpack the conceptual context of its words and sentences. In the end critical questions must be asked about what the text says. This is all the more the case when the text is the Hebrew Scriptures. Beyond unpacking what Genesis says about the origin of the model, we cannot ignore the question, "Is it true?" The answer necessarily is dynamic. At different times and places different claims will be discovered.[1] Furthermore, these claims will be judged differently at different times.[2] In general, some things said will seem to be true, others false, and others doubtful.

---

[1] E.g., several medieval commentators (such as Gersonides), influenced by medieval Platonic and Aristotelian science, uncovered our narrative's use of elements, as well as its atemporal framework. Similarly, some modern commentators (such as Rosenzweig), influenced by modern Kantian and Hegelian philosophy, uncovered our narrative's use of asymptotic functions, as well as its ontological negativity.

[2] E.g., for most medieval philosophical commentators (such as Maimonides), the dynamism of the Creator was conceptually most problematic, since medieval science seemed to demand that God be stable, i.e., not subject to change. Similarly, for most modern philosophical commentators (such as Spinoza), the teleology of the creation was conceptually most problematic, since modern science seemed to demand that the universe be subject solely to mechanical causal principles.

The philosophic disciplines highlighted by the above textual analysis fall into three areas: philosophy of religion, political theory, and scientific cosmology. With respect to the philosophy of religion, assent to Genesis is not easy. Our narrative's strength is that it provides a picture of a physical universe that ultimately is intelligible (1) in terms of purposeful activity, (2) in which the performance of ritual acts are central to what the world means. However, far more difficult to accept is Genesis's claim that everything in the universe exists primarily to serve God, where "to serve" means to offer him food. We tend to consider the notion of divine service to be reasonable only in a metaphorical, spiritualized sense. In contrast, the Hebrew Scriptures, which admit no distinction between the spiritual and the material, understand service to God in literal, physical terms.

More disturbing is our narrative's implicit vision of ideal government. (1) The Hebrew Scriptures tend to associate what is good with separating.[3] In contrast, we tend to identify unification, all other factors being equal, as a moral-political desiratum. (2) The Hebrew Scriptures draw a close analogy between the descriptions of both the nation and the universe as political orders. The order seen to characterize the physical universe that God made functions as an ideal for the order that human beings ought to establish in their world of the political state. Clearly the political model explicitly expressed in our narrative stands in sharp contrast to what most of us believe, viz., that there are fundamental, universal human rights, and that the nation-state exists primarily for the welfare of its citizens. In contrast, clearly the inhabitants of the divine polity of the natural world exist primarily for the sake of its divine ruler, in an order where individual rights have no legitimate place.

---

[3] Conversely, Genesis' account of the tower of Babel (Gen 11:1-9) tends to associate what is bad with unifying. For example, that there was "one language and one speech throughout the earth" (Gen 11:1) strikes most of us as something desirable. In fact, this linguistic unity made it possible for all nations to work together (or, more precisely, to become "a single nation" [Gen 11:6]) in a constructive project to bring "heaven to earth" (Gen 11:4). However, clearly the deity in this narrative places the opposite moral value on this instance of universal political cooperation to advance human good (Gen 11:6ff).

(3) In general, people tend to catalogue the things that occupy the universe as entities, collections of entities, and parts of entities. "Entities" are the things we believe to have independent existence, which, as such, have a right to exist. On the other hand, "collections" are mental constructs, i.e., they are ways that humans collect entities into groups, which, as such, are not real, and hence have no rights whatsoever. In contrast, "parts," unlike collections, exist, but, they exist only as parts, and, as such, unlike entities, have no rights. These distinctions do not turn on facts. For example, we could say[4] that nations are entities, and citizens have identity primarily through (i.e., as parts of) their nations. Similarly, we could say[5] that the ultimate particle constituents of the universe are entities, so that everything larger (including human beings) are mere collections, which, as such, are not real. Finally, it is possible to say[6] that God's universe is an entity, so that everything in it (including human beings) exist only as parts. On all of these alternatives, there is no rationale for a political theory of human rights, and it would seem to be the case that, at least in this one respect, the belief of the aforementioned medieval theologians is true to the intention of the Genesis account of creation.

(4) Implicit in the above problems are two assumptions, viz., (a) what the text says is authoritative, i.e., compels belief precisely because it is said in the Bible, and (b) many of our modern political and religious beliefs are true irrespective of what the Bible says. Neither a traditional Jew nor a fundamentalist Christian nor a secularist would share our concern, since each affirms one but not both assumptions. The problems arise primarily for religious liberals who affirm both assumptions. In this case, to see this text in its historical context would be helpful. If the historical critics were correct, the authors (i.e., the editors) of this text were priests during the Bablyonian exile. From this perspective, what Genesis 1:1-2:3 does is provide a cosmic framework to make sense out of the apparent failure of their lives. These were men who dedicated themselves to the service of God by meticulously performing the ritual sacrifice of the Temple. Now the Temple has been destroyed.

---

[4] As did Ahad Ha-Am and many other late nineteenth and early twentieth century ideologues of nationalism.
[5] As did many ancient Stoics.
[6] As did most medieval Jewish and Christian theologians.

Unquestionably this national tragedy not only called into question the *raison d'etre* of the nation; it called into question their own lives. If God can dispense with the nation Israel, he can dispense with the sacrificial cult, and if he can dispense with that, then there was no real purpose to their lives. The first chapter of Genesis makes cosmic sense out of the sacred service of these priests. It says that there lives were not in vain, that in fact what they did daily was the very reason why the universe exists.

However, if the Genesis account of creation is correct, how could God destroy his Temple? The answer is, he could not, i.e., the destruction is not permanent; the Temple service will be restored. From this perspective, we can infer why the author(s) of the Pentateuch begins the story with creation and brings it to a close with the death of Moses. Creation tells us, the readers, why the universe exists. It exists not to service creatures, but to serve its creator. In fulfilling that service the created world passes through a number of phases. Each begins with birth and ends with death. Each death leads to another, possibly superior phase, in which the events of cosmic history become increasingly focused in greater separation and greater particularity. Hence the phase of universal humanity that begins with the expulsion from the garden of Eden and concludes with the flood, initiates a new phase that begins with Noah, i.e. a sub-set of the general class of the human, and leads to the birth of a single family within that subset, viz. the family of Abraham. The history of that family ends with their enslavement in Egypt, but that tragedy gives rise to a new birth, the creation of the nation Israel with the covenant that Moses brokered with God at Sinai.

Before Moses sings his last song (Deuteronomy 32:1-43) and dies (Deuteronomy 32:49-52), we are told that if the people obey their covenant they will live, but if they do not obey then they will die (Deuteronomy 30:11-20). The full statement of rewards is relatively brief, only fourteen verses (Deuteronomy 28:1-14). In contrast, the full statement of punishments is given fifty four verses (Deuteronomy 28:15-68). Furthermore, while the statement of rewards is vague and fairly innocuous, the statement of punishments is detailed and specific. In fact, it is one of the most powerful (and terrifying) examples of poetry in Western civilization. In other words, the story that begins with creation ends with death and destruction.

How are we to understand this structure? Placing our analysis of creation within the context of priestly authorship during the Babylonian exile provides a clear and powerful answer to the question. Both the authors and their readers know that the nation will choose disobedience and the curse over obedience and the blessing. The blessings can be brief and innocuous because they will not come to be. The curses are detailed and moving because they are more first hand descriptions of what we know occured than moral prescriptions. In fact it is not unlikely that this section of the Torah is a rich poetic statement by people who in fact lived through what they here disguise as the consequences of a choice not yet made. How then are we to understand the structure of the Torah? It is a cosmic myth that uses everything available to its authors — all that they knew of the physical as well as of the humane sciences — to make intelligible a defeat that for them and their nation was felt to be of cosmic proportions.

While this story makes sense of the defeat and suffering of Israel's theocracy, it also provides hope for its future. The world does not exist for humanity; it exists for God. But human existence is not meaningless. Its meaning is to serve God. Life is not about success. Neither is it about happiness. Again, both literally and metaphorically, we are born and we die, and our beginning and our end is solely to serve God. In other words, the Pentateuch explains the death of the nation, and that death account contains a hope, if not a prediction, for a future life — not for the individual, but for the nation. The universe was created to generate an infinite number of particulars, each of whom lives to die, and out of each death arises new, and possibly better (from the only perspective that matters, that of the Creator) life in endless procession towards the one asymptote that is God, that God calls "good."

Finally, in contrast to our conclusions about the implications of this study of Genesis 1:1-2:3 for the humane sciences of politics, and religion, (5) what is most surprising is that the claims uncovered that seem most acceptable are the scientific ones. Of course there are parts of Genesis's picture of the universe whose falsity seems obvious. The most notable example is the location of a region of water above the sky from which, presumably, the rain and mist on earth originates. However, in most other respects the Bible's cosmology is remarkably contemporary. In opposition to the dominant ontology of the religions who claim the source of their tradition in the Scriptures, the Hebrew Scriptures agree with contemporary physics that (1) the "stuff" of the universe is neither mental nor physical. In physics the terms used to express the dynamics of the elemental universe are energy, mass and velocity, all of which are mutually entailing. Similarly, the terms used for fundamental stuff in Genesis are light, dark and spread, all of which also are mutually entailing. Furthermore, Genesis' picture of the origin of the universe (2) as an atemporal model, and not as a description of a first moment in time, (3) that describes the universe as dynamic movements toward an ideal-limit asymptote, (4) whose origin is in something that is not anything, corresponds to the dominance of calculus in contemporary mathematic descriptions of the universe. Similarly, that the picture of the universe is (5) primarily a picture in which the active principle of generation is space corresponds to the dominance of field equations in quantum mechanics in describing particles. *Prima facie,* this kind of mathematics entails that space is not simply the passive abode through which particles pass, but, on the contrary,[7] all things that occupy space are themselves determined by space. Similarly in Genesis, the fresh-life that occupies space lacks concrete specificity. It is ultimately an endless product, through procreation, whose origin is its space. As the generating space of the universe in modern physics are the fields of electromagnetism, weak and strong forces, and gravity, so the originating space of the universe in Genesis are the regions of earth, upper and lower waters, and sky.

The coherence between biblical and modern scientific cosmology suggests that the implications of the biblical text for political science and the philosophy of religion cannot be overcome simply by dismissing the world- and life-view of the Hebrew Scriptures. That biblical science, politics and religion constitute a coherent picture of reality suggests a deep seated incoherence between how modern physical science views the world and what are the standard prescriptions in the humane sciences about ethics. This contemporary incoherence ought to discomfort us. It will not do to continue to isolate these disciplines from each other indefinitely. Because there is only a single, true reality, in the end, we, no less than the author(s) of the Hebrew Scriptures, have to attempt to form some unified picture that can enable us to confront all of reality — the physical and the human — with some degree of coherence.

---

[7] As Plato also asserts in his *Timaeus*.

APPENDIX: AN OUTLINE OF GENESIS 1:1-2:3

Over-all Schema

Day	Created Space	Day	Created Object
1	Day, Night	4	Lighters
2	Sky	5	Swarm (of water), Flier(of sky)
3	Sprout, The Earth	6	Human, Fresh Life (of earth)

Day 7	Created Time	Sabbath

Differentiation of Space

DAY ZERO

DAY ONE

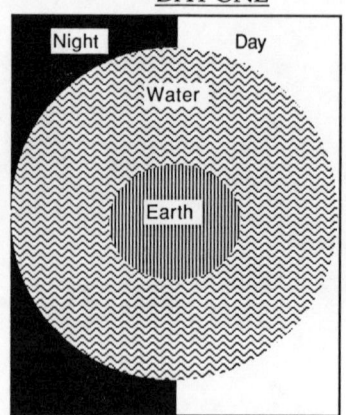

DAY TWO

DAY THREE

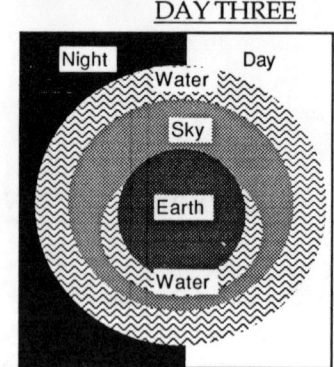

DAY FOUR

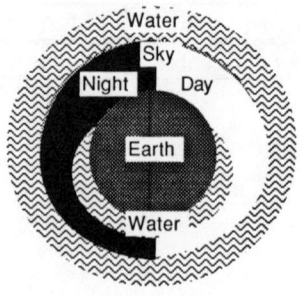

Generation of Occupants of Space

Occupant {type}	Producer	Space	Day/Chpt:vs.	Purpose [Commandment]
sprout {plant, fruit tree}	Earth	Earth surface	3/1:11-12	
lighters {large lighter, small lighter, celestial-objects}	God	Sky	4/1:14-18	Separate light/dark, govern day/night, enlighten earth
swarm {fresh life, flier} {{large sea-serpents, creeper, winged-flier}}	Waters {upper, lower}	Water, Sky	5/1:20-22	(Ful)fill [be fruitful, increase, fill] the space of water; (fliers fly over earth)
Fresh life {creeper, wild animal, domestic animal}	Earth	Earth	6/1:24-25	
Human	God, Earth	Earth	6/1:26-29	(Ful)fill [be fruitful, increase, fill] the space of earth; [conquer and subdue all swarm & fresh life]; (human eats vegetation)

Classification by Value Judgments

	TOV	chpt:vs	KHEN	chpt:vs
1	Light	1:04	The spread separates water	1:07
2	Seas & dry land	1:10	The spread separates seas & dry land	1:09
3	Vegetation	1:12	The earth produces vegetation	1:11
4	Lighters	1:18	The lighters enlighten the earth	1:15
5	Sea- & sky-life	1:21	The water/earth produce life	1:24
6	Land-life	1:25	Life is food for life	1:30

Significance of Verb Forms

	With Consonsant of Conjunction	Without Consonant of Conjunction
Perfect tense	Stable act with limit	Stable act without limit
Imperfect tense	Dynamic act with limit	Dynamic act without limit

Chart of Verb Forms

Day/Chpt.:vs.	Verb	Construction	Subject	Object
0/1:01	gods	1 p	God	The sky, the Earth
0/1:02	is	1 i	The Earth	—
	hovers	3 pt	Wind of God	—
1/1:03	says	1 i w	God	—
	is	1 j	—	Light
	is	1 i w	—	Light
1/1:04	perceives	1 i w	God	The Light
	separates	5 i w	God	The Light, The Dark
1/1:05	names	1 i w	God	The Light
	names	1 p	God	The Dark
	is	1 i w	—	Evening
	is	1 i w	—	Morning
2/1:06	says	1 i w	God	—
	is	1 j	—	Spread

Appendix

	is	1 i	—	—
	separates	5 pt	—	Waters
2/1:07	makes	1 i w	God	Spread
	separates	5 i w	God	Waters
	is	1 i w	—	—
2/1:08	names	1 i w	God	Spread
	is	1 i w	—	Evening
	is	1 i w	—	Morning
3/1:09	tells	1 i w	God	The Waters
	collects	2 i	—	Lower Water
	appears	2 i	Dry Land	—
	is	1 i w	—	—
3/1:10	names	1 i w	God	Dry Land
	names	1 p	God	Seas
	perceives	1 i w	God	—
3/1:11	tells	1 i w	God	The Earth
	sprouts	5 i	The Earth	Sprout
	makes	1 pt	Fruit Tree	Fruit
	is	1 i w	—	—
3/1:12	produces	5 i w	The Earth	Sprout
	seeds	5 pt	Plant	Seed
	makes	1 pt	Tree	Fruit
	perceives	1 i w	God	—
3/1:13	is	1 i w	—	Evening
	is	1 i w	—	Morning
4/1:14	says	1 i w	God	—
	is	1 j	—	Lighters
	separates	5 in	—	The Day, The Night
	is	1 p	Lighters	Signs, seasons, days, yrs
4/1:15	is	1 p	Lighters	Lighters
	enlightens	5 in	Lighters	The Earth
	is	1 i w	—	—
4/1:16	makes	1 i w	God	2 Lighters

4/1:17	places	1 i w	God	Lighters
	enlightens	5 in	Lighters	The Earth
4/1:18	governs	1 in	Lighters	The Day, The Night
	separates	5 in	Lighters	The Light, The Dark
	perceives	1 i w	God	—
4/1:19	is	1 i w	—	Evening
	is	1 i w	—	Morning
5/1:20	tells	1 i w	God	The Water
	swarms	1 j	The Water	Swarm, Flier
	flies above	2 i	Flier	The Earth
5/1:21	gods	1 i w	God	Sea-Swarm
	perceives	1 i w	God	—
5/1:22	blesses	1 i w	God	Sea-Swarm*
	says	1 inf	God	—
	is fruitful	1 im	Sea-Swarm*	—
	increases	1 im	Sea-Swarm*	—
	fills	1 im	Sea-Swarm*	The Waters
	increases on	1 i	The Flier	The Earth
5/1:23	is	1 i w	—	Evening
	is	1 i w	—	Morning
6/1:24	tells	1 i w	God	The Earth
	produces	5 i	The Earth	Fresh Life
	is	1 i w	—	—
6/1:25	makes	1 i w	God	Earth-Life**
	perceives	1 i w	God	—
6/1:26	tells	1 i w	God	The Earth
	makes	1 i	God, The Earth	The Human

Appendix

	subdues	1 i	The Human	The Fish, The Flier, The Domestic Animal, The Land Creeper
	creeps	1 pt	The Creeper	The Land
6/1:27	gods	1 i w	God	The Human
	gods	1 p	God	The Humans†
	gods	1 p	God	The Humans†
6/1:28	blesses	3 i w	God	The Humans†
	tells	1 i w	God	The Humans†
	is fruitful	1 im	The Humans†	—
	increases	1 im	The Humans†	—
	fills	1 im	The Humans†	The Earth
	conquers	1 im	The Humans†, The Earth	—
	subdues	1 im	The Humans†	The Fish, The Flier, The Land Creeper
6/1:29	says	1 i w	God	—
	appoints (food) for	1 p	God	(plants) The Humans†, The Earth-Life
	seeds	1 pt	Plant	Seed
	seeds	1 pt	Fruit-Tree	Seed
6/1:30	is	1 i w	—	—
6/1:31	perceives	1 i w	God	—
	makes	1 p	God	Everything
	is	1 i w	—	Evening
	is	1 i w	—	Morning
7/2:01	finishes	4 i w	The Sky, The Earth, Their Occupants	
7/2:02	finishes	3 i w	God	God's task
	makes	1 p	God	God's task

	rests	1 i w	God	—
	makes	1 p	God	God's task
7/2:03	blesses	3 i w	God	The 7th Day
	sanctifies	3 i w	God	The 7th Day
	rests	1 p	God	—
	gods	1 p	God	God's task
	makes	1 in	God	God's task

Abbreviations for Verb Construction

Conjugation: 1 = simple active; 2 = simple passive; 3 = intensive active; 4 = intensive passive; 5 = causative active; 6 = causative passive; 7 = reflective

Tense: i = imperfect; im = imperative; in = infinitive; j = jussive; p = perfect; pt = participle; w = joined to consonant of conjuction (Waw Consecutive

* Sea-Swarm = large sea-serpents, creeping fresh life that the waters swarm, and winged flier
** Earth-Life = wild animal, domestic animal, creeper of the humus
† The Humans = The male and female human

Appendix

Day/Chpt:vs.	Divine Act	Division*	Object
0/1:02			תהום, חשך, הארץ, תהו ובהו, המים, רוח־אלהים
1/1:03	יאמר־יהי		אור
1/1:04	ירא ויבדל	T_1	האור החשך, האור
1/1:05	יקרא		יום, לילה
2/1:06	יאמר־יהי		רקיע
2/1:07	יעש ויבדל	K_1	הרקיע המים, המים
2/1:08	יקרא		שמים
3/1:09	יקוו יאמר (תראה)	K_2	המים היבשה
3/1:10	יקרא ירא	T_2	ימים, ארץ
3/1:11	תדשא־ יאמר	K_3	הארץ
3/1:12	(תוצא) ירא	T_3	דשא (עשב, עץ)
4/1:14	יאמר־יהי (להבדיל) (היו)		מארת היום, הלילה אתת, מועדים, ימים, שנים
4/1:15	היו...להאיר)	K_4	הארץ
4/1:16	יעש (לממשלת)		המארת הגדלים, 2 הכוכבים היום, הלילה
4/1:17	יתן (להאיר)		רקיע השמים (המארת ב) הארץ
4/1:18	(למשל) (להבדיל) ירא	T_4	ביום, בלילה האור, החשך

Day/Chpt:vs.	Divine Act	Division*	Object
5/1:20	יאמר־ ישרצו		המים עוף שרץ נפש חיה
5/1:21	יברא ירא	T_5	התנינם הגדלים, כל־נפש החיה הרמשת אשר שרצו המים, כל־עוף כנף
5/1:22	יברך...לאמר		אתם (cf vss 20-21)
6/1:24	יאמר־תוצא	K_5	הארץ (נפש חיה: בהמה, רמש, חיתו־ארץ)
6/1:25	יעש ירא	T_6	הבהמה, חית־הארץ כל־רמש האדמה
6/1:26	יאמר..נעשה (ירדו ב)		אדם (בהמה, עוף השמים, דגת הים כל־הרמש על־הארץ, כל־הארץ)
6/1:27	יברא ברא ברא		האדם זכר ונקבה
6/1:28	יברך...יאמר		אתם (cf vs 27)
6/1:29	יאמר נתתי... לאכלה		כל־עשב...על־פני כל־הארץ כל־העץ אשר־בו פרי־עץ
6/1:30		K_6	כל־עוף השמים, כל־חית הארץ, רומש על־הארץ אשר־בו נפש חיה, כל כל־ירק עשב
6/1:31	ירא	T_7 (מאד)	כל־אשר עשה
7/2:1	(יכלו)		צבאם, השמים, הארץ
7/2:2	יכל ישבת...מ		מלאכתו אשר עשה כל־מלאכתו אשר עשה
7/2:3	יברך...יקדש שבת מ		יום השביעי כל־מלאכתו אשר ברא..לעשות

* T = TOV = (It was) good; K = KHEN = (It was) so

Bibliography

Modern Bible Studies

Albrecht, Alt. *Essays on Old Testament History and Religion.* Garden City, Anchor Books, 1968.

Alter, Robert and Kermode, Frank (eds.). *The Literary Guide to the Bible.* Cambridge (MA), Harvard University Press, 1987.

Alter, Robert. *The Art of Biblical Narrative.* New York, Basic Books, 1981.

Anderson, Bernhard W. (ed.) *Creation in the Old Testament.* Philadelphia, Fortress Press, 1984.

Anderson, Bernhard W. *Understanding the Old Testament.* Englewood Cliffs, Prentice-Hall, 1957.

Baab, Otto J. *The Theology of the Old Testament.* New York and Nashville, Abingdon Press, 1949.

Barr, James. *Biblical Words for Time.* London, SCM Press, 1962.

Barr, James. *The Semantics of Biblical Language.* New York, Oxford University Press, 1961.

Barthes, R., Boven, F., et al. *Structural Analysis and Biblical Exegesis.* Pittsburgh, The Pickwick Press, 1974.

Beebe, H. Keith. *The Old Testament: An Introduction to Its Literary, Historical, and Religious Traditions.* Belmont, CA, Dickenson, 1970.

Bentzen, A. *Introduction to the Old Testament.* Copenhagen, G.E.C. Gad, 1962.

Bright, John. *A History of Israel.* Philadelphia, Westminster Press, 1959.

Buss, M.J. (ed.) *Encounter with the Text: Form and History in the Hebrew Bible.* Philadelphia, Fortress Press, 1979.

Buttrick, George A., Bowie, W.R., et al. (eds.) *The Interpreter's Bible.* New York and Nashville, Abington Press, 1952.

Cassuto, Umberto. *A Commentary on the Book of Genesis.* Translated into English by Israel Abrahams. Jerusalem, Magnes, 1961-1964.

Chase, Ellen. *Life and Language in the Old Testament.* New York, Gramercy, 1955.

Chase, Ellen. *The Bible and the Common Reader.* New York, Macmillan, 1952.

Culley, R.C. *Studies in the Structure of Hebrew Narrative.* Philadelphia, Fortress Press, 1976.

Doukhan, Jacques B. *The Genesis Creation Story.* Berrien Springs, Michigan, Andrews University Press, 1978.

Driver, S.R., Plummer, A., et al. (eds.) *The International Critical Commentary.* Edinburgh, T. and T. Clark, 1910.

Eaken, Frank E. Jr. *The Religion and Culture of Israel: An Introduction to Old Testament Thought.* Washington, D.C., University Press of America, 1977.

Eissfeldt, O. *The Old Testament: An Introduction.* New York, Harper and Row, 1965.

Fishbane, Michael. *Biblical Interpretation in Ancient Israel.* Oxford, Oxford University Press, 1985.

Fishbane, Michael. *Text and Texture: Close Readings of Selected Biblical Texts.* New York, Schocken, 1979.

Fox, Everett. *Genesis and Exodus: A New English Rendition with Commetary and Notes.* New York, Schocken, 1983.

Gaster, T.H. Thespis: *Myth, Legend and Custom in the Old Testament.* New York, Harper and Row, 1969.

Gunkel, Hermann. *Schöpfung und Chaos in Urzeit und Endzeit.* s.l., s.n., 1895.

Gunkel, Hermann. *The Legends of Genesis, the Biblical Saga and History.* Translated into English by W.H. Carruth. New York, Schocken, 1964.

Hahn, Robert F. *The Old Testament in Modern Research.* Philadelphia, Fortress Press, 1966.

Hastings, James (ed.). *Dictionary of the Bible.* New York, Charles Scribner's Sons, 1898.

Heidel, Alexander. *The Babylonian Genesis.* Chicago, University of Chicago Press, 1963.

Kaufmann, Yehezkiel. *The Religion of Israel: From Its Beginnings to the Babylonian Exile.* Translated into English by Moshe Greenberg. Chicago, University of Chicago Press, 1960.

König, E. *Theologie des Alten Testaments.* Stuttgart, s.n., 1923.

Kramer, Samuel Noah (ed.). *Mythologies of the Ancient World.* Garden City, New York, Doubleday and Co., 1961.

Bibliography

Kramer, Samuel Noah. *The Sumerians*. Chicago, University of Chicago Press, 1963.

Kuntz, J. Kenneth. *The People of Ancient Israel: An Introduction to Old Testament Literature, History and Thought*. New York, Harper and Row, 1974.

Lambert, W.G. "A New Look at the Babylonian Background of Genesis," in *The Bible in its Literary Milieu* , John Maier and Vincent Tollers (eds.), Grand Rapids, Eerdmans, 1979. pp. 285-297.

Leibowitz, Nehama. *Studies in the Book of Genesis*. Jerusalem, World Zionist Organization, 1972.

Levenson, Jon D. *Creation and the Persistence of Evil: The Jewish Drama of Divine Omnipotence*. San Francisco, Harper and Row, 1988.

Levenson, Jon D. *Sinai and Zion: An Entry into the Jewish Bible*. San Francisco, Harper and Row, 1987.

Long, Charles H. Alpha. *The Myths of Creation*. New York, Collier, 1969.

Neusner, Jacob. *Ancient Israel after Catastrophe: The Religious World View of the Mishnah*. Charlottesville: University Press of Virginia, 1983.

Neusner, Jacob. *Christian Faith and the Bible of Judaism: The Judaic Encounter with Scripture*. Grand Rapids, MI: W.B. Eerdmans Publishing Co., 1987.

Neusner, Jacob. *Judaism and its Social Metaphors: israel in the History of Jewish Thought*. Cambridge and New York: Cambridge University press, 1989.

Neusner, Jacob. *Judaism as Philosophy: The Method and Message of the Mishnah*. Columbia, S.C.: University of South Carolina Press, 1991.

Neusner, Jacob. *The Philosophical Mishnah*. Atlanta: Scholar's Press, 1988.

Neusner, Jacob, and Greeley, Andrew M. *The Bible and Us*. New York: Warner Books, 1990.

Neusner, Jacob, Levine, Baruch A., and Frerichs, Ernest S. (eds.). *J u d a i c Perspectives on Ancient Israel*. Philadelphia, Fortress Press, 1987.

Niditch, Susan. Chaos to Cosmos: *Studies in Biblical Patterns of Creation*. Chico, California, Scholars Press, 1985.

Noth, Martin. *A History of Pentateuchal Traditions*. Englewood Cliffs, Prentice-Hall, 1979.

Noth, Martin. *The History of Israel*. New York, Harper and Row, 1958.

Pedersen, Johannes. *Israel: Its Life and Culture*. London, Oxford University Press, 1926.

Pfeiffer, R.F. *Introduction to the Old Testament*. New York, Harper and Brothers, 1941.

Polzin, Robert. *Biblical Structuralism: Method and Subjectivity in the Study of Ancient Texts*. Philadelphia, Fortress Press, 1977.

Pritchard, James B. *The Ancient Near East.* Princeton, Princeton University Press, 1950.
Rad, Gerhard von. *Genesis, A Commentary.* Translated into English by John H. Marks. Philadelphia, Westminster Press, 1972.
Rosenberg, David. *Congregation.* New York, Harcourt, Grace, Jovanovich, 1987.
Rowley, H.H. *The Old Testament and Modern Study.* Oxford, Clarendon University Press, 1951.
Sarna, Nahum M. *The JPS Torah Commentary: Genesis.* Translation and commentary by Nahum M. Sarna. Philadelphia, Jewish Publication Society, 1989.
Sarna, Nahum M. *Understanding Genesis.* New York, Jewish Theological Seminary of America, 1966.
Schneidau, Herbert N. *Sacred Discontent: The Bible and Western Tradition.* Berkeley, University of California Press, 1977.
Segal, Moses Hirsh. *The Pentateuch: Its Composition and Its Authorship and Other Biblical Studies.* Jerusalem, Magnes Press, 1967.
Sellin, E. and Fohrer, G. *Introduction to the Old Testament.* Nashville, Abingdon Press, 1965.
Speiser, E.A. *Genesis.* Garden City, Doubleday, 1977.
Stadelmann, Luis I.J. *The Hebrew Conception of the World.* Rome, Analecta Biblica, 39, 1970.
Vawter, Bruce. *On Genesis.* Garden City, Doubleday, 1977.
Wakeman, Mary K. *God's Battle with the Monster.* Leiden, Brill, 1973.
Weinfeld, Moshe. "God the Creator in Genesis 1 and in the Prophecy of Second Isaiah" (in Hebrew). *Tarbiz* Vol. xxxvii, No. 2 (Jan., 1968) pp. 105-132.
West, James King. *Introduction to the Old Testament.* New York, Macmillan, 1981.
Wienfeld, Moshe. "Sabbath, Sanctuary and the Kingdom of the Lord" (in Hebrew). *Bet Mikre* vol. 69 (1976/1977) pp. 188-193.
Wright, G. Ernst. *The Old Testament Against Its Environment.* London, SCM Press, 1950.

Rabbinics

Primary

מקראותגדולות. Part I. New York, Pardes Publishing House, 1951.
מדרש הגדול. Margulies, Mordecai (ed.) Jerusalem, מוסד הרב קוק, 1947.

Bibliography

מדרש רבה. Warsaw, 1913. Translated into English by H. Freedman and Maurice Simon. London, Soncinco, 1939. Translated into English by Jacob Neusner. *Genesis Rabbah: The Judaic Commentary of the Book of Genesis, A New American Translation.* Chico, Scholars Press, 1985.

Doron, Pinchas. *The Mystery of Creation According to Rashi: A New English Translation and Interpretation of Rashi on Genesis I-VI.* מוזנים, 1984.

Levi Ben Gershon (Gersonides). פירוש התורה. Venice, Daniel Bomberg, 1547.

Moses Ibn Maimon (Maimonides). דלאלה אלחאירין *(The Guide of the Perplexed)* [מורה הנבוכים]. Translated into Hebrew by Judah Ibn Tibbon. Wilna, I. Funk, 1904. Translated into Hebrew by Joseph Bahir David Kapach. Jerusalem, מוסד הרב קוק, 1972. Translated into French by Solomon Munk. Paris, A. Franck, 1856-1866. Translated into English by Shlomo Pines. Chicago, University of Chicago Press, 1963.

Oles, M. Arthur. "A Translation of the Commentary of Abraham Ibn Ezra on Genesis with a Critical Introduction." Unpublished Ph.D. dissertation. Cincinnati, Hebrew Union College-Jewish Institute of Religion, 1958.

Rashi. *Pentateuch and Rashi's Commentary.* Edited by Abraham Ben Isaiah and Benjamin Sharfman. Brooklyn, S.S.&R. Publishing Co., 1949.

Saadia Ibn Joseph Al-Fayyumi. כתב אמנות ולאעתקאדאת *(The Book of Beliefs and Opinions*) [ספר אמנות ודעות]. Leiden, Brill, 1880. Translated into Hebrew by Judah Ibn Tibbon. Leipzig, C. W. Vollrath, 1864. Translated into English by Samuel Rosenblatt. New Haven, Yale University Press, 1948. Selections translated into English by Alexander Altmann. *The Book of Doctrines and Beliefs.* New York, Atheneum, 1969.

Secondary

Altmann, Alexander. "A Note on the Rabbinic Doctrine of Creation." *Journal of Jewish Studies* VII (1956) pp. 195-206.

Boyarin, Daniel. *Intertextuality and the Reading of Midrash.* Bloomington, Indiana University Press, 1990.

Burrell, David B. & McGinn, Bernard (eds.). *God and Creation: An Ecumenical Symposium.* Notre Dame, Notre Dame University Press, 1990.

Davidson, Herbert. "Maimonides' Secret Position on Creation." In I. Twersky (ed.). *Studies in Medieval Jewish History and Literature.* Vol. 1. Cambridge (MA), Harvard University Press, 1979. pp. 16-40.

Eichler, Barry and Tigay, Jeffrey (eds.). *Studies in Midrash and Related Literature.* Philadelphia, Jewish Publication Society of America, 1990.

Feldman, Seymour. "Platonic Themes in Gersonides' Cosmology." In *Salo W. Baron Jubilee Volume.* Jerusalem, American Academy for Jewish Research, 1975. pp. 383-405.

Feldman, Seymour. "The Doctrine of Eternal Creation in Hasdai Crescas and Some of His Predecessors." *Viator* II (1980): 289-320.

Feldman, William M. *Rabbinical Mathematics and Astronomy.* London, M.L. Cailingold, 1931.

Goldstein, Bernard R. "Levi Ben Gerson: On the Relationship between Physics and Astronomy." *Proceedings of the International Conference on the Interrelationship between Physics, Cosmology, and Astronomy: 1300-1700.* Tel Aviv/ Jerusalem, s.n., 1984.

Goldstein, Bernard R. "The Origins of the Doctrine of Creation *Ex Nihilo.*" *Journal of Jewish Studies* 35 (1984): 127-135.

Goldstein, Bernard R. "The Status of Models in Ancient and Medieval Astronomy." *Centaurus* 24 (1980): 132-147.

Grant, Edward (ed.). *A Source Book in Medieval Science.* Cambridge (MA), Harvard University Press, 1974.

Harvey, W. Z. "A Third Approach to Maimonides' Cosmogony-Prophetology Puzzle." *Harvard Theological Review* 74, 3 (1981): 287-301.

Harvey, W. Z. "Albo's Discussion of Time." *Jewish Quarterly Review* (1981): 220-221.

Harvey, W. Z. "The Term *Hitdabbekut* in Crescas' Definition of Time." *Jewish Quarterly Review* 71 (1980): 44-47.

Klein-Braslavy, S. "Interpretation of Maimonides of the Term 'Create' and the Question of the Creation of the Universe," (in Hebrew) *Da'at* 16 (1986): 39-55.

Klein-Braslavy, S. *Maimonides' Interpretation of the Story of Creation* (in Hebrew). Jerusalem, s.n., 1978.

Lipschitz, A. "The Theory of Creation of Rabbi Abraham Ibn Ezra." *Sinai* 84 (1979): 105-125.

Manekin, Charles. "Problems of 'Plenitude' in Maimonides and Gersonides." In R. Link-Salinger (ed.) *A Straight Path: Studies in Medieval Philosophy and Culture.* Washington, D.C., The Catholic University of America Press, n.d. pp.183-194.

Neugebauer, O. "The Astronomy of Maimonides and Its Sources." *Hebrew Union College Annual* XXII (1949): 322-364.

Neusner, Jacob. *Genesis and Judaism: The Perspective of Genesis Rabbah, An Analytical Anthology.* Chico, Scholars Press, 1985.

Nuriel, A. "Maimonides on Chance in the World of Generation and Passing Away. (in Hebrew)" *Jerusalem Studies in Jewish Thought* 2, 1 (1982/1983): 33-42.

Nuriel, A. "חדוש העולם וקדמותו על פי הרמב"ם." *תרביץ* XXXIII (1964): 372-387.

Rabinovitch, Nachum L. *Probability and Statistical Inference in Ancient and Medieval Jewish Literature.* Toronto, University of Toronto Press, 1973.

Ravitsky, E. "חדוש או קדמות העולם בתורה הרמב"ם." *תרביץ* XXXV (1966): 333-348.

Rosenthal, Erwin I.J. "Medieval Jewish Exegesis: Its Character and Significance" *Journal of Jewish Studies* 9 (1964), pp. 265-281.

Sambursky, Samuel and Pines, Shlomo. *The Concept of Time in Late Neo-Platonism.* Jerusalem, Israel Academy of Sciences and Humanities, 1971.

Saperstein, Marc. *Decoding the Rabbis: A Thirteenth-Century Commentary on the Aggadah.* Cambridge (MA), Harvard University Press, 1980.

Sarfatti, G.B. *Mathematical Terminology in Hebrew Scientific Literature of the Middle Ages* (in Hebrew). Jerusalem, Magnes Press, 1968.

Sorabjis, Richard. *Time, Creation and the Continuum.* Ithaca, Cornell University Press, 1983.

Staub, Jacob J. *The Creation of the World According to Gersonides.* Brown Juadic Studies #24. Chico, Scholars Press, 1982.

Urbach, Efraim E. חז"ל: פרקי אמונות ודעות. Jerusalem, Magnes Press, 1969. Translated into English by Israel Abrahams. *The Sages: Their Concepts and Beliefs.* Jerusalem, Magnes Press, 1975.

Vermes, Geza. *Scripture and Tradition in Judaism.* Leiden, E.J. Brill, 1961.

Weiss Halivni, David. *Peshat and Derash: Plain and Applied Meaning in Rabbinic Exegesis.* New York, Oxford University Press, 1990.

Wolfson, Harry Austryn. *Crescas' Critique of Aristotle: Problems of Aristotle's Physics in Jewish and Arabic Philosophy.* Cambridge (MA), Harvard University Press, 1929.

Wolfson, Harry Austryn. "Emanation and Creation Ex-Nihilo (in Hebrew)." In *Studies in the History of Philosophy and Religion.* Vol. II. Cambridge (MA), Harvard University Press, 1973. pp. 623-629.

Wolfson, Harry Austryn. "Halevi and Maimonides on Design, Chance and Necessity." In *Studies in the History of Philosophy and Religion.* Vol. II. Cambridge (MA), Harvard University Press, 1973. pp. 1-59.

Wolfson, Harry Austryn. "The Meaning of Ex Nihilo in the Church Fathers, Arabic and Hebrew Philosophy and St. Thomas." In *Medieval Studies in Honor of J.D.M. Ford*. Cambridge (MA), Harvard University Press, 1948.

Wolfson, Harry Austryn. "The Meaning of Ex-Nihilo in Isaac Israel." In *Studies in the History of Philosophy and Religion*. Vol. I. Cambridge (MA), Harvard University Press, 1973. pp. 222-233.

Wolfson, Harry Austryn. "The Platonic, Aristotelian and Stoic Theories of Creation in Halevi and Maimonides." In *Studies in the History of Philosophy and Religion*. Vol. I. Cambridge (MA), Harvard University Press, 1973. pp. 234-249.

Wright, Addison G. *The Literary Genre Midrash*. New York, Alba House, 1967.

Philosophy
Primary

Aristotle. *The Works of Aristotle Translated into English*. Edited by W.D. Ross. Oxford, Oxford University Press, 1908-1952.

Cohen, Hermann. *Das Prinzip der Infinitesimal-Method*. Frankfurt a.M., Suhrkamp, 1968.

Cohen, Hermann. *Jüdische Schriften*. Edited by Franz Rosenzweig. Berlin, 1924.

Cohen, Hermann. *Reason and Hope*. New York, W.W. Norton, 1971.

Cohen, Hermann. *Religion d. Vernunft aus den Quellen d. Judentums*. Frankfurt a.M., 1929. Translated into English by Simon Kaplan. *Religion of Reason*. New York, Ungar, 1972.

Cohen, Hermann. *Schriften zur Philosophie und Zeitgeschichte*. Berlin, 1928.

Plato. *Platonis Opera*. Edited by J. Burnet. Oxonii, e typographeo Clarendoniano, 1900—.

Plato. *The Timaeus*. Translated into English by D.M. Cornford in *Plato's Cosmology*. Indianapolis, Bobbs-Merrill, n.d.

Plato. *The Timaeus*. Translated into English by H.D.P. Lee. Baltimore, Penguin Books, 1986.

Plato. *Timaeus, Critias, Cleitophon, Menexenus, Epistles*. Translated into English by R.G. Bury. Cambridge (MA), Harvard University Press, 1929.

Rosenzweig, Franz. *Der Stern der Erlösung*. Frankfurt a. M., J. Kaufmann, 1921. Translated into English by William W. Hallo. *The Star of Redemption*. Boston, Beacon Press, 1971. Translated into Hebrew by Yehoshua Amir. כוכב הגאולה. Jerusalem, Bialik Institute, 1970.

Rosenzweig, Franz. *Franz Rosenzweig: Der Mensch und Sein Werk, Gessamelte Schriften*. The Hague, Martinus Nijhoff, 1976-1979.

Spinoza, Baruch. *Ethics*. Translated into English by W. H. White and revised by A.H. Stirling. 1949.

Spinoza, Baruch. *Opera*. Edited by Carl Gebhardt. Heidelberg, C. Winter, 1972.

Spinoza, Baruch. *The Chief Works of Benedict De Spinoza*. Translated into English by R. H. M. Elwes. New York, Dover, 1955.

Spinoza, Baruch. *The Collected Works of Spinoza*. Edited by Edwin M. Curley. Princeton, Princeton University Press, 1985.

Spinoza, Baruch. *The Ethics and Selected Letters*. Translated into English by Samuel Shirley. Indianapolis, Hackett, 1982.

Spinoza, Baruch. *The Ethics of Spinoza and De Intellectus Emendatione*. Translated into English by A. Boyle. London and New York, 1955.

Spinoza, Baruch. *The Tractatus Theologico-Politicus*. Translated into English by A.G. Wernham. Oxford, Oxford University Press, 1965.

Secondary

Allen, Donald J. *The Philosophy of Aristotle*. London, Oxford University Press, 1970.

Allen, R.E. (ed.). *Studies in Plato's Metaphysics*. New York, Humanities Press, 1965.

Apostle, H. George. *Aristotle's Philosophy of Mathematics*. Chicago, University of Chicago Press, 1952.

Burkert, W. *Lore and Science in Ancient Pythagoreanism*. Cambridge (MA), Harvard University Press, 1972.

Caspar, Bernard. *Das dialogische Denken: Eine Untersuchung der Religionsphilosophischen Bedeutung Franz Rosenzweigs, Ferdinand Ebners und Martin Bubers*. Freiburg, Herder Verlag, 1967.

Claggett, Marshall. *Greek Science in Antiquity*. London, Collier Macmillan, 1955.

Curley, Edwin. M. *Spinoza's Metaphysics: An Essay in Interpretation*. Cambridge (MA), Harvard University Press, 1969.

de Vogel, C.J. "What was God for Plato." *Philosophia, Part I: Studies in Greek Philosophy*. Assen, Van Gorcum, 1970. pp. 210-242.

Dicks, D.R. *Early Greek Astronomy to Plato*. Ithaca, N.Y., Cornell University Press, 1970.

Duhem, Pierre. *Le Système du Monde: Histoire des Doctrines Cosmologiques*. Paris, Libraire Scientifique, 1913.

Eliade, Mircea. *The Sacred and the Profane.* New York, Harcourt Brace Jovanovich, 1959.

Farrington, Benjamin. *Greek Science.* Harmondsworth, Penguin, 1944-1949.

Fox, Everett. "Technical Aspects of the Translation of Genesis of Martin Buber and Franz Rosenzweig." Unpublished Ph.D. dissertation, Brandeis University, 1975.

Friedländer, Paul. *Plato: An Introduction.* Translated into English by H. Meyerhoff. Princeton, Princeton University Press, 1970.

Glatzer, Nahm. *Franz Rosenzweig: His Life and Thought.* Philadelphia, Jewish Publication Society of America, 1953.

Gueroult, Martial. *Spinoza.* Paris, Aubier Motaigne, 1968.

Hallett, Harold F. *Creation, Emanation and Salvation: A Spinozistic Study.* Hague, Martinus Nijhoff, 1962.

Heath, T.L. *Aristarchus of Samos, The Ancient Copernicus.* Oxford, Clarendon Press, 1913.

Heath, T.L. *Greek Mathematics.* Oxford, Clarendon Press, 1921.

Hempel, Carl G. *Aspects of Scientific Investigation.* New York, The Free Press, 1965.

Hesse, Mary B. *Models and Analogies in Science.* Notre Dame, University of Notre Dame Press, 1966.

Horwitz, Gertrude Rivka. "Speech and Time in the Philosophy of Franz Rosenzweig." Unpublished Ph.D. dissertation, Bryn Mawr College, 1963.

Hubbeling, H.G. *Spinoza's Methodology.* Anselm, Van Gaeum, 1967.

Jarrett, Charles. "The Concept of Substance and Mode in Spinoza." *Philosophia* 7 (1977): 83-105.

Keyt, David. "The Mad Craftsman of the Timaeus." *The Philosophical Review* 80 (1971), pp. 230-235.

Kirk, G.S. and Raven, J.E. *The Pre-Socratic Philosophers.* Cambridge (MA), Harvard University Press, 1957.

Kuhn, Thomas S. *The Structure of Scientific Revolutions.* Chicago, University of Chicago Press, 1957.

Loewith, Karl. "Martin Heidegger and Franz Rosenzweig on Temporality and Eternity." *Philosophy and Phenomenological Research* 3 (1942): 53-77.

Luria, S. "Die infinitesimaltheorie der antiken Atomisten." *Quellen und Studien zur Geschichte der Mathematik.* Abteilung B, Band 2, Heft 2, 1932. pp. 106-185.

Martin, Thomas. H. *Études sur le Timée de Platon.* New York, Arno Press, 1976.

Mohr, Richard D. *The Platonic Cosmology.* Leiden, E.J. Brill, 1985.

Neugebauer, O. *A History of Ancient Mathematical Astronomy.* Berlin and New York, Springer Verlag, 1975.

Odebrecht, R. *Hermann Cohens Philosophie d. Mathematik.* Berlin, 1906.

Oppenheim, Michael David. "Taking Time Seriously: An Inquiry into the Methods of Communication of Sören Kierkegaard and Franz Rosenzweig." *Studies in Religion* 7 (1978): 53-60.

Pederson, Olaf and Phil, Mogens. *Early Physics and Astronomy.* New York, American Elsevier, 1974.

Popper, Karl. *Objective Knowledge.* London, Oxford University Press, 1972.

Rahel-Freund, Else. *Die Existenzphilosophie Franz Rosenzweigs.* Leipzig, Meiner, 1933. Translated into English by Stephen L. Weinstein and Robert Israel. *Franz Rosenzweig's Philosophy of Existence: An Analysis of the Star of Redemption.* The Hague, Martinus Nijhoff, 1979.

Sambursky, S. *The Physical World of the Greeks.* Translated into English by M. Dagut. London, Routledge and Kegan Paul, 1956.

Sarton, George. *Introduction to the History of Science.* Baltimore, Carnegie Institute of Washington #376, 1927.

Sayre, Kenneth M. *Plato's Late Ontology.* Princeton, Princeton University Press, 1983.

Solmsen, F. *Aristotle's System of the Physical World.* Ithaca, Cornell University Press, 1960.

Sorabji, Richard. *Time, Creation and the Continuum.* London, 1983.

Strauss, Claude Levi. *Structural Anthropology.* Garden City, Doubleday & Co., 1967.

Taylor, A.E. *A Commentary on Plato's Timaeus.* Oxford, Oxford University Press, 1928.

Toulmin, Stephen. *The Return to Cosmology: Postmodern Science and the Theology of Nature.* Los Angeles, University of California Press, 1982.

Vlastos, Gregory. *Plato's Universe.* Seattle, University of Washington Press, 1975.

Wedberg, Anders. *Plato's Philosophy of Mathematics.* Westport, Greenwood Press, 1955.

Wetlesen, Jon. *The Sage and the Way: Spinoza's Ethics of Freedom.* Assen, Van Corcum, 1979.

Wienpahl, Paul. *The Radical Spinoza.* New York, New York University Press, 1979.

Wolfson, Harry Austryn. *The Philosophy of Spinoza: Unfolding the Latent Processes of His Reasoning*. Cambridge (MA), Harvard University Press, 1934.

<u>Modern Science</u>

Aitchison, I.J.R. and Hey, A.J.G. *Gauge Theories in Particle Physics*. Bristol, England, Adam Hilger, 1982.
Barrow, John D. and Silk, Joe. *The Left Hand of Creation*. New York, Basic Books, 1983.
Barrow, John D. and Tipler, Frank J. *The Anthropic Cosmological Principle*. New York, Oxford University Press, 1986.
Bohm, David. *Causality and Chance in Modern Physics*. New York, Van Nostrand, 1957.
Bohm, David. *Quantum Theory*. New York, Prentice Hall, 1951.
Bohr, Niels. *Atomic Theory and the Description of Nature*. Cambridge, Cambridge University Press, 1934.
Bohr, Niels. *The Physical Principles of Quantum Theory*. Chicago, University of Chicago Press, 1930.
Bohr, Niels. *Physics and Philosophy*. New York, Harper and Row, 1958.
Chaisson, Eric J. and Field, George. *The Invisible Universe*. Boston, Birkhauser, 1985.
Chaisson, Eric J. and Stengers, I. *Order Out of Chaos*. New York, Bantam, 1984.
Cornell, James and Leightman, Alan P. *Revealing the Universe: Prediction and Proof in Astronomy*. Cambridge (MA), Massachusetts Institute of Technology Press, 1982.
Dantzig, Tobias. *Number: The Language of Science*. New York, Free Press, 1930.
Davies, Paul C.W. *The Accidental Universe*. New York, Cambridge University Press, 1982.
Davies, Paul C.W. *The Cosmic Blueprint*. New York, Simon and Schuster, 1988.
Davies, Paul C.W. *God and the New Physics*. New York, Viking Penguin, 1983.
Davies, Paul C.W. *Other Worlds*. London, Dent, 1980.
Davies, Paul C.W. *Space and Time in the Modern Universe*. Cambridge, Cambridge University Press, 1977.
Davies, Paul C.W. and Brown, J.R. *The Ghost in the Atom*. Cambridge, Cambridge University Press, 1986.
DeWitt, B.S. and Graham, N. *The Many Worlds Interpretation of Quantum Mechanics*. Princeton, Princeton University Press, 1973.

Bibliography

Duff, M.J. and Ishon, C.J. (eds.). *The Quantum Theory of Space and Time.* Cambridge, Cambridge University Press, 1982.

Ekeland, Ivar. *Mathematics and the Unexpected.* Chicago, University of Chicago Press, 1988.

Fano, G. *Mathematical Methods of Quantum Mechanics.* New York, McGraw-Hill, 1971.

Ferris, T. *Galaxies.* San Francisco, Sierra Club Books, 1980.

Fine, Arthur. *The Shaky Game — Einstein's Realism and the Quantum Theory.* Chicago, University of Chicago Press, 1986.

French, A.P. and Taylor, E.F. *An Introduction to Quantum Physics.* Middlesex, Nelson, 1978.

Gal-Or, Benjamin. *Cosmology, Physics and Philosophy.* Springer-Verlag, 1981.

Gamow, George. *Mr. Tompkins in Wonderland.* New York, Macmillan, 1940.

Gamow, George. *One, Two, Three ,... Infinity.* New York, Bantam Books, 1947.

Gottfried, Kurt. *Quantum Mechanics Vol. 1: Fundamentals.* Reading, MA, Benjamin/Cummings, 1966.

Guth, A.H. and Steinhardt, P. "The Inflationary Universe." *Scentific American* 250 (May, 1984): 116-128.

Harrison, Edward R. *Cosmology.* Cambridge, Cambridge University Press, 1981.

Hawking, Stephen W. *A Brief History of Time: From the Big Bang to Black Holes.* Toronto, Bantam Books, 1988.

Heisenberg, W. *The Physicist's Conception of Nature.* Wesport, Conn., Greenwood Press, 1958.

Honner, John. *The Description of Nature: Niels Bohr and the Philosophy of Quantum Mechanics.* New York, Oxford University Press, 1988.

Hubble, Edwin. *The Realm of the Nebulae.* New Haven, Yale University Press, 1936.

Kaku, Michio and Trainer, Jennifer. *Beyond Einstein: The Cosmic Quest for the Theory of the Universe.* New York, Bantam Books, 1987.

Mandelbrot, B. *The Fractal Geometry of Nature.* New York, W.H. Freeman & Co., 1983.

Merwin, David. *Space and Time in Special Relativity.* New York, McGraw Hill, 1968.

Munitz, Milton K. (ed.). *Theories of the Universe.* New York, The Free Press/Collier-Macmillan, 1957.

Pagels, Heinz. *Cosmic Code.* New York, Simon and Schuster, 1982.

Pagels, Heinz. *Perfect Symmetry.* New York, Simon and Schuster, 1985.

Peat, F. David. *Superstrings and the Search for the Theory of Everything.* Chicago, Contemporary Books, 1988.

Peebles, P.J.E. *Cosmology.* Princeton, Princeton University Press, 1971.

Prigogine, I. *From Being to Becoming: Time and Complexity in the Physical Sciences.* San Francisco, W.H. Freeman, 1980.

Powers, J. *Philosophy and the New Physics.* London, Methuen, 1982.

Rae, Alastair I.M. *Quantum Mechanics.* Bristol, Hilger, 1986.

Rae, Alastair I.M. *Quantum Physics: Illusion or Reality?* Cambridge, Cambridge University Press, 1986.

Redhead, Michael. *Incompleteness, Nonlocality and Realism: A Prolegomenon to the Philosophy of Quantum Mechanics.* Oxford, Clarendon Press, 1987.

Reeves, H. *Atoms of Silence.* Boston, Massachusetts Institute of Technology Press, 1984.

Shipman, H.L. *Black Holes, Quasars, and the Universe.* Boston, Houghton Mifflin, 1980.

Shu, F. *The Physical Universe.* Mill Valley, University Science Books, 1982.

Silk, J. *The Big Bang.* San Francisco, W.H. Freemand, 1980.

Trefil, J.S. *From Atoms to Quarks: An Introduction to the Strange World of Particle Physics.* New York, Scribners, 1980.

Trefil, J.S. *The Moment of Creation: Big Bang Physics.* New York, Scribners, 1983.

Vilenkin, A. "Creation of the Universe from Nothing." *Physics Letters* B117,25 (1982).

von Neumann, J. *Mathematical Foundations of Quantum Mechanics.* Princeton, Princeton University Press, 1955.

Wagoner, R. and Goldsmith, D. *Cosmic Horizons.* San Francisco, W.H. Freeman, 1983.

Weinberg, Steven. *Gravitation and Cosmology.* New York, Wiley and Sons, 1972.

Weinberg, Steven. *The First Three Minutes.* New York, Basic Books, 1977.

Wheeler, J.A. and Zurek, W.N. (eds.). *Quantum Theory and Measurements.* Princeton, Princeton University Press, 1983.

Whitney, Charles A. *The Discovery of Our Galaxy.* New York, A. Knopf, 1971.

INDICES

GREEK & LATIN TERMS

ARETE 29
HUMUS 116-117, 120
HYLE 61
PNEUMA 21
TELOS 97

HEBREW TERMS

'ALAH 17
ADAM 119-120, 126
ADAM 120
ADAMAH 115-117
ADOM 115
AKHLU 131
AL-HA-ARETZ 66-67
AL-PeNAI 17-18, 97
ASAH 13, 44-45
BARA 11-14, 44-45, 97-98, 146
BeHEMAH 111
BOKER 36-38
CHAYAH 93
CHAYAT HA-ARETZ 114
CHAYTO-ARETZ 111-112, 114
CHOSHEKH 17
DAGAH 124
DAGAT 124
DESHE 64, 67-68
DMUT 122
ECHAD 38
ECHAD 137
ELOHIM 10
ERETZ 15
EREV 36, 37-38
ESEV 65-66, 67-68
ET 14
ETZ PeRI 65-66, 67-68
HA-ARETZ 15-16, 56, 63, 81
HA-MAYIM 21-22, 54
HA-SHISHI 137
HAYeTAH 16
HAYU LI 80
HEVEL 17, 121
HITZTALEM 121
ISH 121
KALEH 142
KASHER 134
KAVASH 133
KHEN 46-48, 56, 81
KI 28
KIVSHUHA 130-131
KOACH 63
KODESH 145
KOKHAVIM 84
KOL 114-115
LA 32, 82
LAIMOR 102, 129
LAKHEM 132
LAYLAH 33-34
Le-HA-IR 80, 87
Le-HAVDIL 87
Le-MAMSHELET 82-84, 87
Le-MINO 66
LIMSHOL 87
MALAKH 14
MALKHUT 83
MAREH 122
MASHAL 133
MAYIM 112
MAZRIYA ZERA 66
MeLAKHTO 142
MEMSHALAH 83
MeOD 136
MeOROT 75-76
MeRACHEFET 22
MIL-U 104-105
MILCHAMAH 145
MO'ADIM 78
NA'ASEH 118-122
NATATI 132-133
NEFESH 94-95
NOTEH 42
OR 26-27
OTOT 77-78
PeRU 104
RADAH 133
RAKIYA' 41-44
REMES 100

REMES 111
RESHIT 8-10, 20
RUACH ELOHIM 19-21
RVU 104
SALACH 146
SHAMAYIM 14
SHANIM 78
SHERETZ 92-93
TADSHE 64
TANIN 99-100
TAVNIT 122
TeHOM 18-19
TeNINIM 99
TEREFAH 134
TINYAN 99
TOHU VAVOHU 16-17
TOTZE 69-70, 109
TOV 28-29, 46-48
TZELEM 121-122
TZELEM 122
TZeVA-AM 139-140
TZILEM 121
TZULAM 121
VA 25
VA-YeHIY 25-26
VA-YeVAREKH 102-103
Ve 15, 70, 123
YA'AS 44-45, 82, 88
YAMIM 57, 78
YAR 27-29
YATSAR 44-45
YAVASHAH 54-55
YAVDEL 30
YeHIY 25, 41
YeKADESH 139, 144-145
YeKAVVU 54
YeKHAL 140-141
YeKHULU 139-140
YEREK 134
YIKRA 13, 31-32
YIRDU 123-124
YIREV 105
YISHBOT 139, 142-143
YISHReTZU 92
YITEN 85, 88
YOM 33-34, 46
YOMER 13, 25, 41, 53-54, 75, 88, 139
ZAKHAH 124
ZARO-BO 66

NAMES AND BOOKS

Ahad Ha-Am 151
Anaximander 20
Anaximenes 20
Aristotle 26, 60-61, 63-64, 149
Aristotle, *De Caelo* 121
Cassuto, Umberto 68
Finney, Ross L. 58
Genesis Rabbah 55, 78, 84, 99, 119
Gersonides, Levi ben 26, 43, 149
Ginzberg, Louis 35
Hegel, Georg Wilhelm Friedrich 149
Heracleitus 20
Ibn Ezra, Abraham ben Meir 26, 28-29, 37-39, 43, 82, 84, 112, 118-119, 124
Kant, Immanuel 149
Maimonides, Moses ben 149
Milgrom, Jacob 146
Nachmanides, Moses ben 26, 29, 39, 43, 63, 65, 84, 112, 119
Newton, Isaac 59, 61
Pfeiffer, Robert F. 68
Plato, *Timaeus* 3, 35, 39, 121, 128, 149, 154
Pythagoras 20
Rabbi Acha 55
Rabbi Aibu 118
Rabbi Ammi 119
Rabbi Berekiah 55, 84
Rabbi Chama Ben Rabbi Chanina 119
Rabbi Chanina 118
Rabbi Hila 119
Rabbi Huna 118
Rabbi Isaac 55
Rabbi Jassi 119
Rabbi Jochanan 84
Rabbi Jonathan 118
Rabbi Joshua Ben Levi 119
Rabbi Joshua of Siknin 119
Rabbi Judah ben Rabbi Simon 43
Rabbi Levi 119
Rabbi Samuel Ben Nachman 118-119

Index

Rabbi Simlai 119
Rabbi Simon 84
Rashi 26, 29, 38, 43, 65, 79, 84, 99, 103, 118, 124
Rawls, John 7
Rosenzweig, Franz 124, 149
Sarna, Nahum M. 42
Saadia ben Joseph al-Fayumi 118-119
Sforno, Obadiah 26, 29, 34, 37-38, 43, 65, 84, 118-119, 124
Spinoza, Baruch 149
Spinoza, *Ethics* 106
Thales of Milos 20
Thomas, George B. Jr. 58
Zeno of Cition 20-21, 30

BIBLICAL NAMES AND BOOKS

Aaron 99
Abel 123
Abraham 141, 147, 152
Ahashuerus 130
Amos 121
Cain 77
Chronicles
  First 130
  Second 83, 121, 130
Daniel 12, 41, 83
David 94
Deuteronomy 8, 16, 19, 22, 99, 141, 152
Ecclesiastes 17
Eleazar 42
Esther 130
Exodus 7, 19, 94, 99, 115, 141
Ezekiel 12, 41, 75-76, 99, 121-122
Genesis 7, 12, 69, 78, 99, 105, 115, 121, 134, 141, 150
Habakkuk 12
Haman 130
Isaiah 8, 16-17, 42, 44-45, 83, 99, 115
Jacob 141
Jeremiah 16, 22, 41, 83, 99, 123, 130
Job 7, 16, 41-42, 99
Joel 64
Joshua 12, 130
Judges 12
Kings
  First 12, 83
  Second 83, 115, 121,-122
Lamentations 99, 115
Leviticus 8, 92, 115
Micah 83, 99, 130
Moses 99, 141, 152
  Death of 152
Nahum 115
Nehemiah 8, 123, 130
Noah 105, 123, 152
Numbers 78, 115, 121, 130
Proverbs 20, 115
Psalms 7-8, 12, 16, 26, 41-42, 83, 92, 99, 121, 123
Ruth 69, 110, 118-119
Samuel
  First 16, 115, 121
  Second 42, 94, 130
Saul 94
Song of Songs 115
Zachariah 115
Zechariah 12, 130

SUBJECTS

Action 63, 86, 88, 136
  Unity of 30, 49-52, 70, 82, 86-87, 98, 113, 126, 137,146
Active 23
Actor 86
Air 20-21, 30, 34
Altar 122
Analogy 83-84
Analysis 7, 149
Ancient Near East 4
Angel 14, 63-64,110, 119, 142
Animal 111-112, 114, 117, 120, 124, 126
  Land 103
  Wild 99
Art 121
Asian philosophy 3
Astronomy 27, 110
Asymptote 105, 127, 135, 149, 153, 154
Attribute 106
Author, Biblical 2

Authority 134
Babylonian Exile 151-153
Beast 111
Best reading 2
Betrothing 145
Birds 47, 96, 101
Birth 152
Blessing 102-103, 106, 129-132, 144
Brute 111
Causation 149
Celestial Objects 98, 100, 112
Christian, Fundamentalist 151
Christians 1
Classification 32-33, 101, 111-114, 124, 127
Collection 151
Command 106, 125, 129-131
   Object and recipient 105-106
Conquering 131
Consellation 89
Creation 11, 98
   Out of Nothing 63
   Second Story 7
Creepers 100, 101, 106, 111-112, 114-115, 117, 120, 124-126
Creeping 100-101
Dark 17-19, 22, 27, 30-34, 37, 39, 45, 48-52, 56, 75-76, 80, 87, 106, 143, 154
Day 28, 33, 38-39, 48, 50, 52, 56, 77-80, 84, 87, 91, 106, 146
   Zero 48, 71
   One 38-39, 41, 43, 45, 48-49, 71, 75-76, 87-88, 102, 106, 117, 132, 137
   Two 48, 51-52, 71, 75, 81, 96-97, 102, 106, 113, 117-118, 132, 137
   Three 50, 52, 67, 71, 81, 87, 88, 102, 106, 113, 117, 132, 137
   Four 50, 82, 87-88, 97-98, 102, 106, 112-113, 117-118, 132-133, 137
   Five 50, 97-98, 102-103, 106-107, 109-110, 113, 117-120, 124-125, 129-132, 137, 144
   Six 50, 73, 101, 103, 107, 109-110, 112-113, 118-120, 124-125, 129-133, 137-138, 144
   Seven 94-95, 97, 137, 139, 142, 144-145

Death 152-153
Deconstruction 1
Definition 101
Depth 18, 22
Destruction 133, 137
Disposition 57, 70, 80, 109-110, 112-113
Dragon 99
Duality of Opposites 23, 27, 32-33, 37, 51
Dynamics 59, 93, 97, 102, 113, 118, 123, 127-128, 133, 136, 149, 154
Earth 15-18, 21-23, 30-31, 33-34, 38-39, 42-44, 49, 50-52, 56, 63-70, 75-76, 80-81, 91-93, 97, 101, 106, 109-111, 113, 117-120, 122, 124-126, 130, 139, 143, 154
Eating 133, 137
Eclipse 79
Electromagnetism 154
Element 20-22, 26-27, 49, 57, 61, 76, 80, 96, 110, 149, 154
End 25, 46, 97, 127-128, 133, 136, 143, 145
Energy 154
Enlightenment 86, 133
Entity 47, 151
Etymology 115
Evening 37-38, 143
Event 85-88, 97-98
Excellence See "Virtue" 29
Existential Operator 46
Farming 116-117
Festivals 78, 89
Figure 122, 126, 128
Filling 106
Fire 20-21, 30, 34
Fish 47, 96
Flier 95-97, 100-101, 103, 105, 110-111, 120, 124, 130
Flood 152
Flying 101, 103, 106
Food 95, 123, 133-134, 140, 150
Force 154
Form 26
Fresh 94-95
Fruit 66-68, 95, 104, 106, 109, 111
Function 88, 127-128
Fundamental Universe 39

Index

Fundamentalist 3
Galaxy 89
Garden of Eden 103, 152
Gardening 120
Generation 102
God 10, 17, 20-22, 25, 27-31, 33, 42, 45, 47, 49-52, 57, 60-61, 63, 72, 79, 82, 87, 91, 97-98, 102, 105-106, 109-110, 112-113, 118, 122, 124-127, 131, 136-137, 142-146, 149
    Action of 31, 38-39
    Corporeality of 28
    Imitation of 128
    Partner of 118-120, 126
    Service of 153
    Wind of 17, 19, 22-23, 30-31, 50, 119
    Work of 120
Godding 125-126, 131
Good See "Value" 46
Good Very 28
Governing 106, 123-125, 128, 144
Government 87-88, 124-125, 136
Governor 123
Grammar
    Adjective 61
    Adverb 129
    Conjunction 79
    Construct State 8-9, 82
    Definite Article 10, 114, 137
    Dual 54, 93, 96, 112
    Gender 112, 126, 128, 130-132
    General Term 98, 114
    Imperative 102, 103-106, 130
    Jussive 25
    Negation 16
    Noun 61, 75, 77, 115
    Number 130
    Passive 54, 139, 140
    Plural 54
    Pronoun 130
        Possessive 111, 114, 140
    Root 9
    Royal We 119
    Singular 67, 112
    Ve 15
    Verb 61, 87
        Conjugation 12, 22, 25, 27, 30, 37, 41-42, 44, 54, 64, 69, 76, 83, 85, 92, 94, 97, 102, 104-105, 111, 122-123, 127-130, 132, 139-140, 142, 144
        Imperfect Tense 25, 27, 29-31, 44, 46, 54, 64, 69, 76, 85, 92-93, 97, 102, 118, 123, 127, 129, 133, 139, 142, 144
        Perfect Tense 16, 25, 97, 127, 132
        Waw Consecutive 25, 29, 44, 46, 85, 93, 97, 102, 123, 127, 129, 133, 139, 142, 144
Gravity 154
Ground 116
Happiness 153
Heaven 14
History 109, 128, 144-145, 147
Holy 145
Hope 153
Human 7, 12, 38, 62, 68, 75, 88-89, 102-103, 105, 112, 116, 122-126, 130-134, 137, 144-146
    Uniqueness of the 126-128
Humanity 153
Ideal 57, 70-71, 85-87, 89, 136
Idolatry 121
Image See "Figure" 122, 128
Individual 112, 115, 136, 150
Infinity 93, 106, 118, 123, 136
Intellect, Separate 26, 110
Interpretation 3
Israel 128, 143
    Land of 62, 143, 145
Israelites 62
Jerusalem 62
Jews 1, 151
Jubilee 143
Judaism 1
Labor 94
Land 52, 63, 129-130
    Dry 55-56, 67, 70, 81, 91, 102, 106, 113, 115-118, 125
Language 61, 150
    Narrative 30
Law 32, 88
Leviathan 99
Levites 62, 147
Liberal 151
Life 92-93, 117, 125, 134, 154

Life Form See "Living Thing" 64
Light 19, 26-34, 37, 39, 41, 43, 45, 47-52, 53, 56, 70, 75-76, 80, 87, 91, 102, 106, 117, 143, 154
Lighter 76-77, 79-88, 91, 97, 100-102, 106, 110, 112-113, 117-119, 132-133, 143, 146
Limit 29, 93, 118, 123, 127-128, 136, 145, 154
Linguistic Analysis 2
Living Thing 50, 64, 91, 94, 101, 103, 105-106, 109-114, 118, 122, 124-125, 130-131, 136
Making 97-98, 114, 126, 146
Martyrdom 145
Mass 60-61, 154
Material 14
Mathematics 3, 34-36
   Calculus 34, 57-59, 154
   Field Equations 154
   Geometry 57-59
      Circle 58
      Sphere 59
   Multiplication 104
   Number 38
   Zero 16, 17, 34, 58-59
Matter 60-61
Meat 95
Messenger 146
Messianic Age 79, 136
Methodology 1-4
Midrash 26, 35, 118
Military 140, 145
Mind 94
Mode 106
Model See "Paradigm" 3, 60-61, 70, 72, 77, 79-80, 84, 98, 109, 112-113, 120, 122, 135, 144, 147, 150
Moon 76, 82-83, 87, 89, 98, 100-101
   New 79
Morality 29, 47, 56, 85-88, 128, 133, 135, 150
Morning 37-38, 143
Motion of the Same 39
Myth 153
Names 69
Naming 31-32, 52, 56-57, 60
Nationalism 151
Negation 18

Negativism 4, 121-122, 131, 133, 141, 149, 154
Night 33, 48, 50, 52, 56, 77, 80, 84, 87, 91, 106, 146
Nothing 4, 16-18, 22-23, 27, 32, 39, 48, 53, 57, 146
Object 56-57, 68, 70-71, 79, 87, 135
   of Action 49
Observance 143
Occupant of Space 62, 72, 88, 93, 101, 106, 110, 124-126, 128, 132, 136, 140
Ontology 23, 32, 46-48, 60-61, 64, 94, 106, 121-122
Origin 93, 101, 117, 127-128, 133, 136, 146
Ornithology 101
Paradigm 67-68, 112-113, 115, 117, 122, 127
Part 151
Passive 23
Perceiving, See "Seeing" 28
Perishable 122
Persönlichkeit 124
Pesach 79
Phenomenology 1
Philosophical 7
Philosophy
   Medieval 110
   of Religion 150, 154
   Religious 4, 150
Physics 1, 57-60, 64, 84, 154
Plant 66-67, 70, 95, 111
Political Science 1
Politics 83-84, 86, 98, 120, 124, 128, 132-134, 136, 140, 146, 150, 154
Positivism 4
Postmodernism 1
Potentiality 77, 80, 85-87, 93, 102, 109, 130
Priests See "Levites" 62, 123, 147, 151
Private Property 143
Producing 109-110
Prototype See "Paradigm" 70, 72, 109, 112-113, 115, 122, 132
Purpose 77-79, 82, 86, 88-89, 112, 143, 149-150
Quality 101

Index

Quantity 101, 104
Quantum Mechanics 154
Rabbis 34, 60, 63-65, 78, 84, 99, 103, 118, 136
Rain 153
Reality 32-33, 88, 98, 136-137, 154
   Degrees of 121-122
Red 115
Reproduction 92, 96, 103, 106-107, 113, 120, 130-131, 136, 144, 147, 154
Rest 94
Rights, Human 150-151
Ritual 79, 121, 143
   Jewish 45
Rosh Ha-Shanah 79
Sabbath 38, 50, 62, 79, 86, 94-95, 102, 142-143
Sabbatical 143
Sacrifices 78
Sanctifying 145
Saying 32
Science See "Physics" and "Quantum Mechanics" 26, 135, 150, 153-154
Sea Serpents 100-101, 111, 124-125
Seas 39, 52, 56-57, 63, 67, 70, 81, 91, 102, 106, 113, 117-118, 124-125, 129
Seasons 78
Secularist 151
Seed 66-67
Seeing 27-28, 57, 135
Semites 147
Separation 30, 32-33, 45, 48, 60-62, 79, 85-88, 91, 133, 137, 143, 145, 150
Signs 78-79
Size 93, 101
Sky 15-16, 39, 42-44, 48, 50, 52, 56, 76, 84, 97, 101, 106, 119-120, 124-125, 139, 154
Snakes 99-100, 103
Soil 116
   Virgin 117
Something 27, 53-54
Soul 94, 110, 119
Space 4, 14, 18, 21-23, 30, 33-36, 38-39, 42, 48, 50, 54, 55, 57, 60-63, 71-72, 75-77, 80-81, 83-84, 86, 88, 93, 96-98, 101-102, 105-106, 110, 112-113, 119, 122, 124-127, 130, 132, 136, 145, 154
Species 66
Speech Act 25, 41, 53-55, 62, 75, 82, 91, 109, 113, 117-118, 126, 132, 139, 145
Sphere 110
Spiritual 14, 94
Spread 43, 45, 47-49, 52, 53, 56, 70, 75-76, 80, 86, 96-97, 101, 106, 113, 117-118, 154
Sprout 64, 65-67, 91-93, 95, 106, 111, 117-118, 120
Stability 25, 46, 88, 97, 102, 127-128, 133
Staff 99
Stars See "Lighter" 26, 50, 84
State 88
State-of-Affairs 47, 68, 85-87, 113
Stoics 151
Substance 60-61, 63, 106
Sun 26, 33, 36-38, 76, 82-83, 87, 89, 98, 100-101
Swarm 95, 98, 100-103, 105-106, 109, 111, 113, 118, 120, 124-125, 131
Swarming 109-110
Swimming 97, 111
Temple 62, 78, 140, 145-146
   First 151-152
Theology 4
Tiamat 19
Time 13, 29-30, 33, 37-39, 62, 72, 77, 80, 85-86, 93-97, 109, 112-113, 135-137, 141-145, 149, 154
   Future 144-145
   Past 144-145
Tower of Babel 150
Tree 96
Truth 5, 46-48, 56, 68, 85-87, 135, 149
Tyranny 123, 131
Unity 138, 150
Universe 37, 125, 146
Universe Purpose of 152
Value 16, 22-23, 28-29, 46-48, 62, 87, 102, 117, 121, 123, 128, 131, 135, 145
   Human 114, 117, 128

Vectors 60, 79
Vegetation 62-65, 68, 80-81, 88, 102, 109-111, 113, 116-118, 132, 134
Veil of Ignorance 7
Velocity 154
Virtue 29, 57, 128, 135
Walking 111
Water 18-23, 30-31, 33, 39, 42-45, 48-52, 54-56, 63, 75-76, 80-81, 91-93, 96, 98, 101-102, 105-106, 109-111, 113, 117-120, 125, 131, 139, 153-154
Wilderness 16
Wing 101
Wisdom 20
World-To-Come 26
Worship See "Ritual" 89, 121, 140, 143, 146, 150
Years 79

South Florida Studies in the History of Judaism

240001	Lectures on Judaism in the Academy and in the Humanities	Neusner
240002	Lectures on Judaism in the History of Religion	Neusner
240003	Self-Fulfilling Prophecy: Exile and Return in the History of Judaism	Neusner
240004	The Canonical History of Ideas: The Place of the So-called Tannaite Midrashim, Mekhilta Attributed to R. Ishmael, Sifra, Sifré to Numbers, and Sifré to Deuteronomy	Neusner
240005	Ancient Judaism: Debates and Disputes	Neusner
240006	The Hasmoneans and Their Supporters: From Mattathias to the Death of John Hyrcanus I	Sievers
240007	Approaches to Ancient Judaism: New Series Volume One	Neusner
240008	Judaism in the Matrix of Christianity	Neusner
240009	Tradition as Selectivity: Scripture, Mishnah, Tosefta, and Midrash in the Talmud of Babylonia	Neusner
240010	The Tosefta: Translated from the Hebrew: Sixth Division Tohorot	Neusner
240011	In the Margins of the Midrash: Sifre Ha'azinu Texts, Commentaries and Reflections	Basser
240012	Language as Taxonomy: The Rules for Using Hebrew and Aramaic in the Babylonia Talmud	Neusner
240013	The Rules of Composition of the Talmud of Babylonia: The Cogency of the Bavli's Composite	Neusner
240014	Understanding the Rabbinic Mind: Essays on the Hermeneutic of Max Kadushin	Ochs
240015	Essays in Jewish Historiography	Rapoport-Albert
240016	The Golden Calf and the Origins of the Jewish Controversy	Bori/Ward
240017	Approaches to Ancient Judaism: New Series Volume Two	Neusner
240018	The Bavli That Might Have Been: The Tosefta's Theory of Mishnah Commentary Compared With the Bavli's	Neusner
240019	The Formation of Judaism: In Retrospect and Prospect	Neusner
240020	Judaism in Society: The Evidence of the Yerushalmi, Toward the Natural History of a Religion	Neusner
240021	The Enchantments of Judaism: Rites of Transformation from Birth Through Death	Neusner
240023	The City of God in Judaism and Other Comparative and Methodological Studies	Neusner
240024	The Bavli's One Voice: Types and Forms of Analytical Discourse and their Fixed Order of Appearance	Neusner
240025	The Dura-Europos Synagogue: A Re-evaluation (1932-1992)	Gutmann
240026	Precedent and Judicial Discretion: The Case of Joseph ibn Lev	Morell
240028	Israel: Its Life and Culture Volume I	Pedersen
240029	Israel: Its Life and Culture Volume II	Pedersen
240030	The Bavli's One Statement: The Metapropositional Program of Babylonian Talmud Tractate Zebahim Chapters One and Five	Neusner
240031	The Oral Torah: The Sacred Books of Judaism: An Introduction: Second Printing	Neusner

240032	The Twentieth Century Construction of "Judaism:" Essays on the Religion of Torah in the History of Religion	Neusner
240033	How the Talmud Shaped Rabbinic Discourse	Neusner
240034	The Discourse of the Bavli: Language, Literature, and Symbolism: Five Recent Findings	Neusner
240035	The Law Behind the Laws: The Bavli's Essential Discourse	Neusner
240036	Sources and Traditions: Types of Compositions in the Talmud of Babylonia	Neusner
240037	How to Study the Bavli: The Languages, Literatures, and Lessons of the Talmud of Babylonia	Neusner
240038	The Bavli's Primary Discourse: Mishnah Commentary: Its Rhetorical Paradigms and their Theological Implications	
240040	Jewish Thought in the 20th Century: An Introduction in the Talmud of Babylonia Tractate Moed Qatan	Schweid Neusner
240041	Diaspora Jews and Judaism: Essays in Honor of, and in Dialogue with, A. Thomas Kraabel	Overman/MacLennan
240042	The Bavli: An Introduction	Neusner
240043	The Bavli's Massive Miscellanies: The Problem of Agglutinative Discourse in the Talmud of Babylonia	Neusner
240044	The Foundations of the Theology of Judaism: An Anthology Part II: Torah	Neusner
240045	Form-Analytical Comparison in Rabbinic Judaism: Structure and Form in *The Fathers* and *The Fathers According to Rabbi Nathan*	Neusner
240047	The Tosefta: An Introduction	Neusner
240048	The Foundations of the Theology of Judaism: An Anthology Part III: Israel	Neusner
240049	The Study of Ancient Judaism, Volume I: Mishnah, Midrash, Siddur	Neusner
240050	The Study of Ancient Judaism, Volume II: The Palestinian and Babylonian Talmuds	Neusner
240051	Take Judaism, for Example: Studies toward the Comparison of Religions	Neusner
240052	From Eden to Golgotha: Essays in Biblical Theology	Moberly
240053	The Principal Parts of the Bavli's Discourse: A Preliminary Taxonomy: Mishnah Commentary, Sources, Traditions and Agglutinative Miscellanies	Neusner
240054	Barabbas and Esther and Other Studies in the Judaic Illumination of Earliest Christianity	Aus
240055	Targum Studies: Volume One: Textual and Contextual Studies in the Pentateuchal Targums	Flesher
240059	Recovering the Role of Women: Power and Authority in Rabbinic Jewish Society	Haas
240061	The First Seven Days: A Philosophical Commentary on the Creation of Genesis	Samuelson